G000269974

A Sevenoaks Camera

GORDON ANCKORN

A Sevenoaks Camera

Sevenoaks, Westerham
and surrounding villages
in old photographs

ASHGROVE PRESS, SEVENOAKS

Published by
Ashgrove Press
25 Quakers Hall Lane
Sevenoaks, Kent

©Gordon Anckorn 1979

ISBN 0 906798 00 0

First published 1979

Photoset by Wordsmith Graphics
Street, Somerset
Printed by White Crescent Press Ltd.
Luton, Beds

Contents

Foreword

It is difficult for people of this modern age to exercise the imagination needed to take them back to a past in which they never participated. It is equally difficult to lead them there with words.

In looking through this small book the reader must try to forget modern technology and imagine the world he knows without it. Imagine Sevenoaks in the context of some of the earliest pictures. See the High Street, indeed, most of our roads as merely hard packed dirt as they were when I was a youngster.

Remember, too, that the shops were primitive. Wood was the material of which they were made — often painted green or dark brown. There was no chromium; no plastic; no patent clean surfaces. The counters had to be scrubbed each day and, even then, crumbs and dirt could never be completely banished from subtle cracks in the woodwork.

Food was largely displayed without the benefit of covering. Meat was usually hung on display racks outside the shop, completely uncovered.

Think of a world without the internal combustion engine. No cars, lorries, delivery vans, motor cycles, mopeds, aeroplanes or electric vehicles.

People walked to work, many of them travelling several miles there and back. Any serious travelling was by horse-drawn transport. Tradesmen used carts of various kinds. There were small traps for individuals, larger vehicles for families, even larger coaches for long distances and huge carts, drawn by shire horses for carting trees or the material for road making.

Imagine the effect of a horse and rig bowling merrily along the High Street. Clouds of dust rose from the fast turning wheels, eventually settling on the meat outside the butchers' shops and penetrating into the most carefully protected home.

In winter, the dust was not so acute but mud from the un-metalled roads was a real problem. Cartwheels threw up dirt and water over pedestrians despite any care the driver might exercise.

Sometimes straw was laid over the filth and in summer time a water cart sprayed the main roads to lay the dust.

Almost every house or shop had a small foot-grille let into the front, near the door, on which dirt could be removed from boots prior to the wearer's entrance. Men and women wore boots — the ladies' buttoning from top to instep. Everyone had a button hook — a small, often ornate, hook which was shoved through the button hole, hooked over the button and pulled back through the hole.

Many of the photographs in this book show a subtle 'class distinction' in headgear. The lower classes wore cloth caps. The 'middle class' and rich folk were crowned by top-hats and 'stove-pipes'. The richer, the higher!

Readers might be puzzled at the apparent woodenness of everyone in the early pictures but there is an important reason for this. It exemplifies the speed, or, rather, the lack of it, with which things had to be done.

We think nothing of seeing a coloured photograph emerge from a modern camera within a couple of seconds of it being taken, but realise how different things were a hundred years ago.

The earliest photographs were taken on pieces of glass coated at the time of taking with sensitive material.

The photographer carried his darkroom with him — a thing of black cloth on bamboo framing with a red window sewn into the cloth.

His camera was a box with a lens at one end and a water-tight compartment at the other. The camera was focussed by poking the lens through a light-tight opening in the darkroom; the operator then coated his plate with light-sensitive silver salts, poured off the surplus and quickly placed the plate at the back of the camera, having covered the lens with a cap.

As this 'plate' was nothing like as sensitive as our modern films, a long exposure had to be given to any picture, even in bright sunlight. If there were any people within the field, they had to be asked to co-operate by standing perfectly still while the plate was exposed — hence the wooden attitudes. A boy, often an apprentice, had to run here, there and everywhere to stop people in their tracks.

One wonders at the patience of such 'victims' until it is realised that photography in its youth was a very magical thing. To be immortalised by this new art-form was a privilege.

Sevenoaks has had many professional photographers. Undoubtedly the Essenhigh Corke family has left us more records than others because while they did a great trade in portrait photography, they also went out into the field and photographed the places of Sevenoaks and district.

Charles Essenhigh Corke had a studio where Howard King, and later his son George, carried on business in our own times. Then there was Wallis and Barton of 74 High Street, Brunton, of London Road, the Cranbourne Studios, Ernest Fielder of St John's, Morrell Campbell of the High Street, J.H. Jewell and F.G. Benson of Westerham and a host of others, all of whom have left examples of their work.

In earlier times the photographer was usually an artist in his own right and often a taxidermist to boot. In certain cases, artists were photographers who saw the virtue in the camera which could give them a 'thumb-nail' picture from which they could paint their own picture in the comfort of the studio.

One such man was A.H. Norwood who had a small studio in Oak Hill Road, Sevenoaks. He was adept with a half-plate camera, and carried out every process of development in his own darkroom.

Another artist-photographer was Mrs W. Hawkins of Barnfield, Chipstead Common. She used a small camera with which to take 'notes' — painting her pictures in her own inimitable style and finishing them from her photo-references in her home. All these people have left records of the Sevenoaks of years ago.

I began collecting photographic records of Sevenoaks and district in the early thirties. Some were my own or those of my contemporaries, but others were those of such people as the Essenhigh Corkes, the Bruntons, the Jewells, the Bensons and the picture makers who started it all.

As time went on and old records became more difficult to find, I practised various methods of copying faded photographs, even applying infra-red or ultra-violet light. I acquired a fair amount of expertise in this field and eventually preserved more than 1000 photographs which otherwise would have been lost to us.

The men at the municipal refuse tips were my closest allies. They recovered scores of old pictures which had been thrown away and kept them until my fairly regular visits.

Many were dreadfully defaced or damaged. These had to be carefully washed, ironed or pressed and finally mounted and filled with dental plaster. After restoring absent pieces, these were photo-copied and printed.

The whole collection will eventually be preserved in Sevenoaks — perhaps, I hope, the public library.

Perhaps the greatest contribution to the more modern history of the area has been provided by my erstwhile colleague Mr Alex Watson, Chief Photographer of the *Sevenoaks Chronicle,* some of whose pictures are reproduced. To him, and all the photographers who ever exposed a glass plate to leave a record of our Town and Locality, I offer our grateful thanks.

Introduction

I was born at South View, Barrett's Road, Dunton Green 66 years ago, the son of W.L. Anckorn, journalist and poet, and the grandson of W.J. Anckorn of Arbroath, one of the most eminent photographic pioneers of the day. His pictures won awards in salons all over the world and he was patronised by many 'crowned heads'.

It was a strange world into which I was born and one which indelibly impressed itself on my memory.

Perhaps the first thing which I remember was seeing the soldiers hauling massive guns behind teams of six and eight horses, into the field opposite our home. I believed the Germans were coming to Dunton Green!

Eventually I made friends with some of the men. I remember being lifted on to the barrel of a huge gun from which lofty perch I watched them carrying out loading and firing drills.

In those far-off days there were soldiers everywhere. My parents often invited the men to 'smoking' evenings which consisted mainly of song. *There's a Long, Long Trail Awinding, Pack up Your Troubles in Your Old Kit Bag* and other popular war tunes are burned on my memory. A young officer, Bill Clayton, became my God-father. For the short time I knew him I idolised this handsome soldier. He was killed in France within a year.

Sevenoaks was one of those areas near London to which wounded soldiers were brought from the fields of Flanders. The Cornwall Hall was converted into a hospital. Chipstead Place was similarly transformed and it was to this place that came scores of Belgian wounded. The walking cases were so designated by having to wear a blue 'wounded' suit.

One wounded Belgian soldier was Matthieu des Jardins. He was a constant visitor to our home. After a long convalescence he was posted back to the trenches with little prospect of being other than 'cannon fodder'.

After the war, my father went to Belgium to investigate the story of Nurse Cavell (executed by the Germans as a spy), for his paper. I was taken with him and, as we passed through Liège, we saw a Gendarme standing on traffic duty in shirtsleeves, munching an enormous loaf-sandwich — occasionally emphasising his directions by brandishing this unusual comestible at the motorists.

He turned as we walked by and, to our amazement and delight, he was our Matthieu. The sight of a policeman embracing my father with tears in his eyes was, to a young boy, something to remember.

Matthieu posted himself 'off duty' immediately and took us home. I have never seen a celebration like it because the whole village turned out when they heard the news and made it a kind of civic event.

I still have a small flag which was once owned by Edith Cavell. It was given to my father by her aide, Madame Bodart.

That war did one thing for me. It gave me a passion for aeroplanes. My first aircraft was bought for me by my parents at Rye. It was propelled by pedals and had a wingspan of five feet. I used to ride it on the London Road and everywhere. Nobody minded because the carts could easily drive round me.

Many years later I achieved my greatest ambition by gaining my pilot's certificate. Since that time I have logged many hundreds of pilot-hours at Rochester, Croydon and Biggin Hill — mostly taking photographs of the Sevenoaks scene from the air.

Talking of Sevenoaks and aircraft, a strikingly clear picture in my mind's eye is of the occasion when my father took me to Sevenoaks Vine to see a fighter 'plane take off. It was, I believe, a Sopwith Pup and it was there to help a 'help the soldier' week appeal.

There was a massive crowd which waited with bated breath for the great moment of take-off. Willing hands dragged the frail looking machine to the corner of the field by the pavilion and held on to the wings and tail. A mechanic spun the prop' and the engine caught with a puff of blue smoke and the never-to-be-forgotten smell of castor oil.

The God-like creature in the cockpit waved to us, gunned the throttle and was off, skimming lightly over the Vine, just clearing the trees and the Vine Tavern to disappear, like a mote, into the sky. He came back, briefly, to give a demonstration of aerobatics, and then was gone — leaving at least one child with a burning desire to fly one of those beautiful machines.

It is difficult, these days, to remember the world before television, the telephone, electric light, refrigerators, radio and sophisticated forms of travel. It is a sobering thought that when the oldest pictures in this book were taken, electricity was hardly a serious consideration, and it was almost thirty years after the photograph of the cattle in Sevenoaks High Street was taken before the first 'signalling through space without wires' was achieved and wireless was here to stay.

Our wonders, as children, were the things of the countryside. We walked into the fields and woods, finding pleasure in adapting what we found for playthings. We made whistles from the Fool's Parsley stems, catapults from the Spindlewood forks.

The sound I can still hear in my memory is the hammer on the farrier's anvil. It came from everywhere as one passed from village to village — a rhythmic clang clang as pure as the great hunk of metal from which it rose. Our farrier worked behind the Duke's Head pub. There was another at Riverhead behind the White Hart, another at the foot of Tub's Head and several more in the town. One which still remains is that in Old Post Office Yard. Old Man Terry was there in the old days. His son Bill followed him and it is now owned by Mr W.E. Pearce, still 'family', who was an armourer during the war.

One of the wondrous things I learned as a boy watching the farrier was how to make a great explosion. If you brought iron from the fire glowing hot, then spat on the anvil, and quickly placed the iron over it, giving it a great blow with the hammer, the result would bring the soot from the rafters and make the iron and tins ring in sympathy. They said, with the conviction of their natural knowledge, that it was the instant expansion of the steam and the compression of the blow which made the noise.

The natural noises of the Smithy seemed to blend with the noises from the fields; the cattle sounds and the soft grinding of the cart wheels passing along the dirt-bound London Road.

We heard, at regular intervals, the muffin man's bell or the toffee man's cry. The rag man was never far off with his "Any old rags" and toy balloons as reward for cast out materials. We marvelled at the skill of the men who mended chairs or rivetted broken china, sitting on the grass outside the house performing little miracles of repair. The tinkers came quite regularly to mend the pots and pans which had lost handles, or developed leaks. They all worked for a shilling or two.

Every village had its several slaughter houses where local butchers and even the odd 'amateurs' killed their cattle or pigs. The conditions were rough and insanitary but the meat was sweet and tender after hanging. Quick freezing was unknown.

The bakeries were places to linger by, for the smell of the new bread was exotic. Every village had its quota of bakers, each with his own method of baking — secrets handed down from father to son. The big bread companies with their steam baking were unknown.

All the tradesmen had delivery carts — swift high-built vans drawn by good horses which visited the customers on their daily rounds. In the advertisements of the time one could read the words under most advertisers' notices 'Families waited on Daily'. Mr A.S. King of the Vine Dairy 'Waited upon Families Three Times Daily' with dairy goods from the Sevenoaks Common Farm, and stated that he kept special cows for 'the Nursery and Invalids'.

Most people employed colza oil or paraffin for lighting their homes but, by the time of my early memories, the wealthy folks were getting gas generator plants and, later, electric generator sets. Water was pumped from wells and stored in public reservoirs but many people relied on what came off the roofs into great stone underground tanks. We could draw up the water at any time and watch the little wriggly things swimming about. Of course, all the water which came into the tap over the sink was taken through a series of gauze filters.

Kids played, mostly in the London Road. That was a real playground until motor cars and chars-a-bancs started tearing through our villages at great speeds up to twenty miles an hour.

We had 'seasons' for our various games — top whipping, hoop bowling, kite flying. When our Saturday penny had been carefully spent we made tops from cotton reels, hoops from bamboo and kites from newspaper or brown paper.

One toy, very dear to me, was a banger, made from a key, nail and piece of string. The key was tied to one end of the string the nail to the other. Red headed match heads were scraped and the stuff wedged into the shank of the key. The nail was then pushed into the key to compress the chemical and when the machine was swung by the string against a wall, the resultant detonation was music to a small boy's ears. I was 'cured' of this addiction by my father, after blowing his deed-box key to pieces.

The days of my youth were the steam age days and, although we hardly noticed the gradual redundancy of horses, 'steamers' and, just as insidiously, motor cars took over the business of transport.

Even farming relied largely on steam engines. Great machines which made the very ground on which they stood vibrate, and the atmosphere around them pulse with their gentle but compelling power drove the threshers and even the ploughs.

For this latter function a contractor would position a steam engine at each side of the field to be ploughed. An eight-furrow plough was then drawn from one side to the other, alternately, the engines advancing a set distance after each traverse. The plough was drawn by a steel hawser, power-wound round drums hung under the belly of the steam engines.

On the roads, steam rollers and traction engines displayed their power. With the coming of the Foden and the Sentinel engines (the latter having the boiler transverse, like today's Minis) the speed of steam increased enormously, and inflated tyres superseded the original artillery type wheels.

I was an inquiring lad and I learned a thing or two about steam engines on wheels. One concerned static electricity.

During its running, a steamer became highly charged with electricity, being completely insulated from 'earth' by rubber tyres devoid of graphite. The normal practice was to have a chain dragging along the ground to bleed the static off but, if the driver forgot, or for his own reasons wanted the charge to be stored up, the chain was lifted.

Touching the machine in such circumstances was a painful and frightening thing because the whole charge would immediately run to earth with a bright flash and a loud crack, giving the unfortunate person the fright of his life. Policemen seemed to be the target for such whimsy. Drivers would often pull up to ask directions and policemen would invariably touch the cab when talking to the driver. The result was a police force that knew all about static.

Very often the chain would really be forgotten and when it was, it fell to the crew of the engine to get the benefit of the invigorating discharge as their feet touched the ground after a run.

It was still the era of the gentry in Sevenoaks. Today, that word has acquired a mocking connotation but the people who lived in the great houses were, more often than not, aristocrats who took a vast pride in their homes and estates. Many of them regularly disbursed large sums of money to charity.

Perhaps the most controversial of these was Sir Edward Meyerstein, a Jewish member of the London Stock Exchange who lived in Morant's Court at Dunton Green.

A shrewd man, he yet had a great feeling for people in trouble. There was not a man who appealed to him for help in vain if his story was true.

Meyerstein was a millionaire. There were few in those far-off days. He decided to do something for Dunton Green to convert it from a cluster of working-type cottages straddling the road to London.

His plan was to widen the road by setting back the homes on one side and re-building them and providing thatched roofs. The first to be converted were the cottages in Shab Hall Road (re-named Morant's Court Road), where the road turns just before the Morant's Court bridge which now spans the by-pass. Meyerstein turned what were mean ship-boarded hovels into what can be seen there today and it was this type of home that he would have provided for the village. Nobody could see where the 'catch' lay, however, and they turned the scheme down with such phrases as 'We don't want a New Jerusalem in Dunton Green.' There was no catch. Sir Edward only wanted to be the benefactor of his neighbourhood and to share the worldly goods with which he had been endowed by his labours and his good fortune.

He sought to benefit Sevenoaks Hospital a year or two later but, there again, his motives were thought suspect. At the time, Dr Gordon Ward and the Hospital Management Committee were at loggerheads. Meyerstein sought to resolve the 'row' by re-instating the status quo.

He offered the hospital, then desperately asking for funds for their extension and re-building scheme, £10,000 — a vast sum in those days — if they would revert to the original committee which included Ward.

The administrators refused to accept the money with 'strings'. Meyerstein gave the money, and more than twice that amount later, to the Middlesex Hospital.

Of the other owners of great mansions round Sevenoaks, Francis Crawshay was one of those characters who live in memory and the imagination. He was the owner of Bradbourne and a man surrounded by mystery and, if truth was known, by a certain amount of superstitious fear.

Crawshay was a Welsh iron Baron who owned coal mines and iron foundries. He came to Sevenoaks to live and it was at Bradbourne that he caused great stone monoliths and Druidic circles to be erected within the grounds. Their esoteric significance kept the superstitious 'locals' out of the grounds after dark.

He was a man who believed in universal benificence and charity but the thing for which he was remembered, long after his death, was the great Bradbourne Bell.

Crawshay had this massive one ton bell cast in one of his foundries. On it were complete details of his family. The women viewed it with disgust as their birthdays were there and all the world could see how old they were.

The bell was sounded religiously at 6 a.m., noon and 6 p.m. — the time being checked with London — and it was heard clearly as far as Riverhead, Dunton Green and Seal.

Crawshay was buried at Brasted. His grave is some 20 yards to the north of the entrance and is interesting because its surround is cast iron and contains certain objects of druidical symbolism.

Bradbourne House was eventually demolished by the famous Syd (watch it come down) Bishop of Orpington who bought it for its material value.

Another beautiful local mansion was the Wildernesse, bought before the turn of the century by Sir Charles Mills, Bt., later Baron Hillingdon. After his death the place was sold and became the Wildernesse Club. This was a country club of enormous proportions which included a magnificent ballroom, a famous stairway, several tennis courts and one of the finest golf links in the country.

The golf club survives. All that has altered is the disposition of the first three holes and the fact that the clubhouse is now a place apart from the great house. That is now a home of blind children and their tutors and is called Dorton House.

Greatness House once stood not all that far away, on the site of the present Greatness playing fields. It was a grim looking fortress of a place outside, but had an interior of great splendour. It was built by the Nouaille family whose silk mills, in Mill Lane, produced the finest silks, some of which were used by Royalty on state occasions. Little is known of the house apart from its somewhat ignoble end. It was blown up by a film company during the making of a war film.

Montreal, at Riverhead, built by Jeffrey Amherst, was actually constructed from the ragstone blocks of which the hospice of St John at Bat and Ball was made. When

Montreal was eventually demolished, these blocks were again used, this time to build the walls round the new houses on Montreal estate.

Nobody really knows where the hospital of St John was located but it is generally held that it must have been close to where the Bat and Ball railway station eventually made its appearance. On ancient maps there is still the evidence of its possible location by the name of 'Spital Field' at Bat and Ball.

The local events which made a deep impression on my mind are not necessarily those which have found their way into the history books, yet they have their own importance.

For instance, there was the great performance of John Moisant, who flew the Channel for the first time carrying a passenger. This flight, because of its circumstances, stirs my imagination and, I believe, should have been hailed as an achievement greater than that of Bleriot because it was in an identical aircraft yet carrying twice the load.

John Moisant was an American of Spanish descent who became obsessed with flight. He made his attempt to cross the Channel less than a year after Bleriot's successful achievement. He was a complete novice: he undertook this perilous journey the third time he had ever piloted an aircraft. It was in 1910 that he and his mechanic, named Fileux, took off from Paris to fly to Calais and then on to Dover. I have delved back into as many records as I could find after discovering a battered old photograph of his aircraft, marked on the back with the words 'Crash at Kemsing'.

In all, I managed to find seven photographs of Moisant, his flight and the various events which marked it. I also found part of his propeller, two of his autographs and a couple of pictures of the kitten, named Miss Paris, that was said to have been carried by him from France as a mascot. In fact, the animal was given to him at Dover and was looked after at Kemsing by a local girl.

Moisant had nine forced landings and two serious crashes during his epic flight and that at Kemsing was the most serious. It occurred at Cotman's Ash, on the hill above St Clere. The airframe and propeller were broken and while repairs were being made a propeller was to be brought from France. The *Daily Mirror*, however, who were carefully watching this important flight, managed to get a replacement from an aviator using the same type. When ready to take off, Moisant was asked by Sir Mark Collet, who had given him shelter during his stay, to fly round the back of the house if possible, so that his wife, an invalid confined to bed, could see an aeroplane for the first time. Moisant obliged but in doing so a wing hit an oak tree, bringing the aircraft back to earth in another very bad landing.

Moisant crashed or force-landed again at Shoreham, before finishing his flight at Beckenham, having failed to find the field at Crystal Palace designated by the nervous authorities.

Another event in our area which will be remembered for its drama and loss of life, was the train disaster at Riverhead in 1927. It sticks in my mind because it was the first encounter I had with anything so terrible, but also because I was given the job of running 'copy' from the scene to Sevenoaks by the then Editor of the *Chronicle*, Mr J. Kirkwood Browne.

It was the worst rail tragedy ever to have occurred on the Southern Railway. It happened at about 5.30 p.m. when a down train, hauled by a 'River' type loco, went off the tracks and hit the Shoreham Lane bridge. Parts of the train were hurled several hundred yards, the bridge was severely damaged and thirteen people lost their lives. Scores of injured were lying all over the banks when I ran to the spot. I remember the engine lying on its side with the steam gently rising from its broken pipes. I remember the cries of the injured and the awful confusion as local people tried to ease their hurts and prepare them for transport to hospital.

I particularly remember a photo-newsman going up and down the line photographing the dead. So much feeling against him was roused that it was a wonder he was not attacked. The police had to make a statement saying that he was taking pictures for them to expedite identification. I even remember his name — John Barton. He was killed a few months later in an air crash.

My life has been touched, in some measure, by flight. As a youngster the cost of flying was prohibitive to someone earning the equivalent of 50p a week. The only way was to take a 'five bob' flight with the barnstormers who toured the country giving flights to all and sundry.

I think I flew with them all, particularly with Sir Alan Cobham who regularly visited the old airfield at Sundridge, traversed by the Chevening road. I cycled to Penshurst aerodrome each week-end to get a free flight in an old Spartan, as wages for cleaning down the aeroplanes. I even flew with Pauline Glover, the famous woman aviatrix, who was giving flights at Turvin's Farm, Dunton Green. Since that time I have flown with such celebrated 'circuses' as the Black Arrows, Blue Diamonds, Red Arrows and the 56 Lightning Squadron aerobatic team. On several occasions I was in a cockpit of one of the formation teams flying at the Farnborough Airshow — a fantastic privilege.

One of my oldest friends, Ted Sawyer, has loaned me a picture of Alan Cobham's most unusual aircraft, the Flying Flea, which is reproduced in this book. We flew with Cobham in 1928 as kids. It was, therefore, not inappropriate that Ted was the brave 'guinea-pig' who volunteered to be the human ballast when, at the old Croydon airport, I took my certificate for passanger carrying.

The Sundridge airfield may well have been an emergency 'back-up' for Biggin Hill but its origin is obscure. It was equipped with hangars (now farm buildings) which were, at one time, used as the garage for the West Kent bus service which did faithful duty in Sevenoaks and district before the State decided the fate of all private bus companies.

These hangars recall another local character, and I hope he will take no offence at this description, Mr Tom Worsell, who still lives in the town.

He was a keen aviator who flew with the Cinque Ports Aero Club. He had an engineering workshop on the north side of Bradbourne Vale Road in which he made machines, mended other people's broken bits and pieces, and even did gunsmith work. There seemed to be nothing he could not make or mend. In his lifetime he has been a writer, accomplished pilot, electronics expert and radio 'ham', who built his own radio station — G3BGU — and was in constant contact with like people all over the world.

My most exciting recollection of Tom was when he built his own aeroplane in the Sundridge hangars. It was registered as G-EAWS and used a Singer 10 h.p. motor car engine for motive power. I was there when he got it off the ground but, alas, it hit a ditch on landing, turned turtle and was smashed.

Living in Dunton Green as a boy, my early memories are tinged by that area.

The village was bounded on the south by Hamlin's Mill and Bog's Island — as they named the area of Pounsley, because of the flooded shanty town of huts used by the miners brought there for the excavation of the railway tunnels.

Where Hodder's great book centre now stands, Harvey Frost, the local garage owner also tended the huge steam engine which provided the village with water from a great well shaft. The shaft must still be there, under Hodder's front lawns, but domed over when the pumping station disappeared.

Sevenoaks was our 'market town' and the family would go there on Saturdays. The market was still a feature at that time — the stalls being on either side of the High Street outside the Chequers. As kids, we enjoyed going to Franks' iron-mongery, where all sorts of intriguing household articles were on display.

Payne's grocery store, where the Sun Do restaurant now is, was equally astonishing, especially at Christmas time. Plum puddings, crackers, spices, root gingers, and cheese produced an amalgam of scents which made the mouth water. I remember my parents being allowed to taste any of the cheeses displayed before buying. Plastic film, quite apart from the expense, has done away with this custom today.

We went to Buckwells for our coffee. It is still roasted and ground there today. My mother invariably went to Marchant and Wrights for cotton and ribbons. My delight there was in watching the lady in the little wooden kiosk in the centre of the shop receiving and disbursing money and change with the singularly clever overhead rail system actuated by little rubber powered catapults. The customer's money was put into a little round container and shot to the cashier who returned the bill, marked 'paid', with the change, by the same means.

There were few shops below Bligh's Hotel. Suffolk Terrace, if you will glance at the photographs of the area, was a quiet row of dwellings whose occupants were mostly professional people. A doctor lived in one, a dentist in another. There was a small school at the south end, run on expensive lines by a local woman.

I can still remember some of the water places — relics of the days before piped water in Sevenoaks. One was at the Arboretum near the turning into Argyle Road, another at the foot of Six Bells Lane and, of course, the Fountain provided drink for the thirsty, in thick iron cups anchored to the stone by stout chains.

Water was of prime importance to the steam engines which abounded on the roads round Sevenoaks and places were provided for the replenishment of tanks. Most hills had troughs at the summits where horses and steamers could drink but the natural sources all had their 'sumps' into which hoses could be dropped.

There was one at Morewoods, by what is now the police station. Here the little stream flowed towards the Bradbourne Lakes from Brittain's Farm where the whole frontage was a clear lake on which scores of water fowl paddled. There was another at Longford — part of the stream which came down from the Montreal lakes, via the spouts in the Montreal wall at Riverhead Square, under the road and on to the Bull-finch. A wooden roller was provided in the square on which to roll the suction hose to the water to fill the engine tanks. That little stream also provided water for the tanyard opposite Linden Square and the water-cress beds between there and the Bullfinch. It then meandered through Baden Powell's gardens and into the Long Ford, now overbuilt by the Marley factory. It ended by joining the Darent at Hamlin's Mill.

Fire fighting was an inexact science in the early days. Most villages had their own fire fighting apparatus to try to contain the flames until the 'Ready' brigade from Sevenoaks had made the journey, the fire engine being horse-drawn. It reminds me of an incident perhaps half a century ago when Dunton Green brigade was called into action.

Our fire 'shed' was carefully placed out of harm's way under an oak tree at the side of the Parish Room. I never saw any of the apparatus used but, peeping through the cobweb covered windows, I could see the contents — a two wheeled handcart containing several buckets, an oil lamp and some hosepipe tied up in rolls.

One day we had a storm and a bolt of lightning ran down the tree and hit the fire station, igniting it.

There was pandemonium. Several volunteers tried in vain to open the door but the padlock was too much for them. The key was in the pocket of the Captain, Mr Lusted, in London. He was a city businessman as well as the Captain of the fire brigade and Chairman of the Working Men's Club.

Somebody tore off, on a bicycle, to Riverhead where a similar shed was located but, incredibly, a tree had established itself outside the door and the fire cart could not be pulled out.

Riverhead eventually gave its fire apparatus to Dunton Green, preferring, no doubt, to rely on the services and better resources of the U.D.C. fire brigade.

During the construction of the Sevenoaks by-pass I was instrumental in discovering an ancient burial ground. Having once read that, when Polhill was originally turned at the junction of Otford Road, several skeletons were unearthed, I was waiting when the contractors started removing chalk from this spot to form the Polhill entrance into the by-pass.

It was not long before I spotted a bone sticking out of the cliff. A kindly digger driver hoisted me aloft in his bucket and I eventually dis-interred eight skeletons from the path of the machines. My digging, however, proved an embarrassment and a team of 'emergency' diggers from the Maidstone museum came out. They uncovered a battlefield burial ground and, nearby, a Saxon graveyard.

At this spot, it is said, Canut fought a bloody battle with the soldiers of Edmund Ironside in 1016. But my story is not a history and those who would read more of the Polhill story should go to Maidstone, where the record and the relics are on view.

I must also mention, in the context of archaeology (of a kind), that I also had a major part in the founding of a world-war-two museum. This was the Halstead War Museum, the Curator of which is Mr Ken Anscombe. Without touching on some of the incredible stories we encountered in the dis-interring of some 200 crashed Battle of Britain aircraft and the collecting of some 16,000 exhibits, I would say that the museum is one of the most important of them all. It was featured on Nationwide and several T.V. programmes, in the *Daily Telegraph Supplement* and in practically every national paper and, by being the first in this country to use a mine-detector to locate 'buried treasure' we were probably the first to spark off the Treasure Detector cult in Britain. The Museum still exhibits in Halstead and also in the North of England.

But these are my own recollections. Browse through the pages to follow. See Sevenoaks and its villages as they were many decades ago.

Whatever your mood, it is an eternal truth that the view always seems better while looking back over your shoulder.

Sevenoaks Street Scenes

1   An unusual photograph, taken in the early part of this century.
Unusual, because it shows a corner of Essenhigh Corke's studio with
some of his work exhibited on the wall of what became S. Young & Son's
large store. Corke was the man whose artistry left the greatest record of
the town in its early years. On the opposite side of the road was
A. Baker's shop — a combined sweet shop and café, baker and
tobacconist's. The Bakers were probably one of the oldest families in
Sevenoaks. Originally plumbers, they came to the area when the roof of
Knole was restored — most of the lead work was done by the Bakers.
The shop remained in the hands of the family until the 1960s, the last
shop being called Sevenoaks Supplies in which Rayner Baker, a former
Pathfinder pilot, was a familiar figure.

2   One of the few remaining photographic records of the Shambles area of
Sevenoaks. This was taken about 1865 and shows part of the original
Dorset Inn before it received its 'face lift' and false front. In the early
part of the 18th century the pub was the Pied Bull to set it apart from the
other Bull Inn (later the Royal Oak). Before that it was the Swan Inn,
holding a good deal of surrounding land. According to some records the
Pied Bull was the scene of Jack Cade's rebellious fighting after the battle
of Solefields.

   The shop on the corner opposite was that of George's butchers, and it
is still a butcher's shop today. The shop on the extreme right was
originally the town jail which, today, has been charmingly restored by
Dale Johnson and is used as a modern furniture shop.

3 The Royal Crown Hotel was a going concern long before Sevenoaks was anything more important than a place to stop during the arduous coach journeys from London to the coast. It was old, even when the Yankees were fighting the battle of Gettysburg.

A self-supporting hotel of quite lavish proportions, it eventually became the social centre of Sevenoaks with its massive ballroom and 'luxury' bars.

Behind the hotel were beautiful gardens in which guests could sun themselves. Lower down into the South Park slopes, there was a miniature farm where pigs were bred, chickens roamed free and vegetables were produced for the hotel kitchens. There was even an aviary for the interest of the guests.

The photograph which appears on the cover of this book is one of the oldest records of the Royal Crown, dating from approximately 1859. Many famous people stayed there, including Henry Irving and Dame Ellen Terry.

4 Part of the beautiful gardens of the Royal Crown Hotel where afternoon teas for 1s 6d could be had during the summer months. From this spot, now the Focus Cinema car-park, there was in those days an uninterrupted view of the Downs.

5   Hitherto unpublished, this photograph taken by a Mr Stanger shows the backlands which now constitute the greater part of Rockdale Old People's Home. St Nicholas's Parish Church dominates this 1870 scene, and the old Rectory can be seen with its lavish and formal gardens. That Rectory was demolished some 20 years ago. It had become the home of giant fungi and rising damp to such an extent that demolition was forced on those who administered it.

6   An early photograph of Lime Tree Walk, originally a small footpath between South Park and the London Road which was developed by the building of what were then artisans' cottages. The architects made so good a job of their design that these houses have survived the best part of a century and are much in demand today as substantial town dwellings.

On the left of the picture can be seen the signboard of the Lime Tree temperance hotel, one of the most popular haunts of the Cycling Clubs of London and the home of the Sevenoaks Cycling Club. At the turn of the century, Lime Tree Walk was visited almost every week-end by scores of 'Penny Farthing' bikes, tricycles and the new 'safety' pedal cycles. Timberlake, the bike builder, had a shop at the entrance to Lime Tree Walk, (now Hoads) where he sold custom-made cycles. His premises, originally, were those of the Sevenoaks Penny Bank — the first in Sevenoaks.

7 One of the earliest photographs of the London Road, probably taken about 1860, which shows Hely & Co's carriage works on the left. This quite celebrated works had been turning out carriages and wheeled vehicles of every description since 1799 as well as capes, cape-hoods and canopies. They built the Lime Tree Studios as their paint shop. In that building, where now are stairs, was a steep ramp up which the carriages were drawn to be given their final treatment in a dustless atmosphere.

On the right can be seen the plain wooden building that was the premises of Mr Barton, Corn Chandler. It was in this building that many of the old pictures in this book were developed by Essenhigh Corke, who established his dark rooms and studio here.

8 This lovely Christmas-time picture looks just a bit too modern in a history book but it was actually taken in 1900 (the year we coined the term 'hooliganism', derived from a London gang called Hooley — hence Hooleygangism — who excelled in street fighting; Sir Samuel Hoare formed a committee to combat the new form of rowdyism).

To return to the London Road of the time, we can see the end of S. Young & Son's shop and Barton's corn chandlery where Essenhigh Corke and later Howard King had their photographic studios. Caslake's cycle shop lay a little farther towards the top of the hill, and where Daws' store now stands was Hely's carriage works. The object in the road behind the cart was a gas lamp standard.

9 An incredible Tub's Hill reminiscent of a country lane at its worst, typical of the 1860s when this picture was taken. At that time Bligh's hop gardens were the only feature on the east side of the hill. On the left of the photograph can be seen the iron railings which guarded the children of the St Nicholas's Infants school while, at the extreme end of the line of buildings was the Arboretum with its huge walnut tree and public well. Drivers of carts had to fit an iron shoe to the wheels to make them skid, rather than turn, while negotiating the difficult slope.

10 Tub's Hill, named so in honour of a pub at the foot, called the Tub's, has had so little to offer aesthetically, that very few photographs of it exist. This picture, dated about 1920, shows the Post Office (left) then operated by H. Moore, F. Waller's general store which sold everything from tobacco to cycle tyres, a few anonymous shops and then the Sevenoaks Motor Car company's garage.

On the right is part of Tye's garage. In the distance can be seen Whitehead's masonry works and shop. The cart, negotiating the space between the two cars, belonged to Mr Parris who operated a bakery in the High Street. In the far distance, left, we can just see the sign of one of the early Sevenoaks pubs — the Rock and Fountain which was also a local 'doss-house'.

12 After the First World War, Sevenoaks was still but a small town with few commuters. Despite the fact that most traffic was horse-drawn, the motor car was here to stay. The ubiquitous Model T. Ford was as popular here as anywhere else. I well remember (with considerable pleasure and nostalgia) learning to drive on one of these machines. Mr Albert Packman of Dunton Green allowed me to accompany him on his rounds as a fishmonger and eventually to drive the Ford under his expert tuition.

This picture shows Sevenoaks station and parade in the days of the Model T. Note that the road has not yet been metalled.

11 Few pictures illustrate so starkly the growth of an area as much as this well preserved photograph of Granville Road. On the left can be seen the overhang of what is now the railway but the cutting had barely been made when the scene was like this. Knott's Mill had not long disappeared and the view over the great chalk pit at Dunton Green was practically devoid of buildings.

13 It is almost impossible for those who have not reached middle age to imagine that this photograph was taken on the busy A25, and almost in Sevenoaks. A close look at the house, however, shows that it is the Bottle Cottage which still stands almost dead opposite Lambarde Road on the Bradbourne Vale Road between Bat and Ball and Riverhead. The gentleman with the 'safety' bike puts a date to the photo. It was taken in about 1910.

14 This picture shows Bat and Ball as it was in the early days of motoring. It is quaint to remember the busy A25, one of the worst traffic roads in Kent, when it was merely a dirt packed cart route flanked with cornfields as can be seen here, looking west. On the right, by the triangular danger sign, can be seen the roof of Tom Worsell's workshop. Tom was (and still is) a man who could always make or mend anything that had beaten a lesser mechanic. On this spot he kept his own aircraft. A skilled pilot, he originally flew from Lympne.

15 You might think this picture a little dreary, but it is one which records a phase in the life of the hospital at Sevenoaks. The original cottage hospital was little more than a cottage with facilities. This was extended in 1903, re-built in 1921, and had a children's ward added in 1927. The first extension was to have been a memorial to King Edward VII but the war deferred this.

After the war, a great appeal was made for £28,000 with which to build a proper place where patients and accident cases could be properly treated. Part of the money was also to provide the Vine war memorial (costing about £800). The money was eventually found but not without some acrimony and bad feeling within the organisation. Because of this, Mr Edward Meyerstein, later Sir Edward, withdrew his offer of a gift of £10,000. In this picture we have the original hospital (left) and the first extension, plainly seen to be new brickwork.

16 An unusual aspect of Sevenoaks High Street about 1925. It shows the original Electric Cinema run by Mr Robinson (also proprietor of the Royal Oak hotel). It was the latest thing of its kind with Western Electric 'wide Range' equipment and was open daily from 2.30 p.m. The prices of admission ranged between 6d and 2s 4d. There were three other picture houses in Sevenoaks about this time, the Carlton on St John's Hill, the Majestic cinema in London Road and the town's original picture house on Station Parade.

As a small boy, I assisted the proprietor of the Station Parade cinema by taking turns at cranking the projector — an arm-aching task relieved only by reversing the movement when the owner (Mr Usher) was in another part of the building re-winding. The roars of laughter from the auditorium as the film went in reverse gave the game away. In the auditorium, May Weth 'ad-libbed' on the violin and Claud Hunter on the piano to suit the action of the film.

17 A sight to nonplus the motorist of today, indeed. Cows mooching aimlessly down the High Street at milking time. The time is about 1900 and the 'ladies' are on their way from Bligh's Farm to the meadows at the top of St Botolph's. If an occasional 'horseless carriage' came their way, it would have to wait until they had walked the length of the High Street. It is interesting to see, in the background, the old Club Hall which adjoined the Constitutional Club. This provided room for most of the dances and entertainments in Sevenoaks. It was an unlovely Victorian building, perhaps, but until demolished by a German bomb it played an important part in the social life of the town.

18 A strangely deserted High Street, this, showing what today is the Electricity Board's showroom, Goodrich's and the Bank. This photograph was taken in 1901, and shows the dusty dirt road with its open drains and cobbled entrances. In this stately row were mainly professional people — doctors, dentists and a small school for the children of gentlefolk.

19 This is probably one of the most astonishing pictures of the collection. It shows two quite ordinary oast houses and a barn — admittedly of great proportions. It is their siting which causes amazement because they were at the top of Pembroke Road where it joins Sevenoaks High Street. The photograph is unique in that no other photographic record exists of this scene.

Today, Oastfield Court stands here, a mute endorsement of the history of the site by Dr Gordon Ward, whose home it was, and who was an eminent local historian.

The oasts were part of Bethlehem Farm on which grew the hops which John Bligh cultivated and brewed into Sevenoaks beer.

20 Perhaps the only industry found in Sevenoaks in olden times, apart from basket-making and the fashioning of carts and wagons, was that of brewing. There are many records of local ale-houses where home beer was brewed but Sevenoaks had important breweries such as that of A. Smith & Co, John Bligh and William Humphrey Golding.

This picture shows Smith's Brewery. It stood at the north end of Suffolk Place, on the site later occupied by the Electric Cinema (subsequently the Granada). To the north of the building can be seen what became the premises of Merlins, the builders' merchants. Between the two sites were, originally, massive and lengthy malting houses. In the old days, with the two chimneys of Smith's brewery going strong and those of John Bligh, only a few hundred yards to the south, the air of Sevenoaks was strangely exhilarating, say those who remember.

21 Telling the history of Sevenoaks more dramatically, perhaps, than any other, this photograph of more than 100 years ago shows the entrance to the yard of Bethlehem Farm on the west side of Sevenoaks High Street. It is difficult to believe that this is today the entrance to the main car park and 'bus station of Sevenoaks. The barns were on the site of what is now the Co-operative store.

22 A fine photograph of Bligh's Hotel at the turn of the century. A baker's cart and a family trap are the only traffic to pass through this otherwise quiet place. Somebody's gardener is quickly reaping the the rewards of horse-drawn traffic in the distance. It was 'good for the roses'.

23 A look at this photograph, taken about 1903, seems to breathe tranquillity. Elegant ladies walk along the side-walks opposite Bligh's Hotel past which an artisan carrying his tools in a bag on his back walks to or from his work. Bligh's brewery entrance is at the end of the wall and Mr Amos Pett's basket shop can just be seen a little farther on. The only traffic is horse drawn and we can just see a Victoria coach drawing out from Buckhurst Lane.

24 An extremely old photograph of Sevenoaks High Street, showing Bligh's Hotel on the left and Suffolk Place on the right. Beyond Bligh's can just be seen the remnants of Bethlehem (or Bedlam) Farm, protected by stone walls. Just round the corner, in Pembroke Road, were two of John Bligh's hop kilns. A faint outline, beyond, is Pond Cottages which flanked a large and noisome pond — still remembered by a few with long memories.

On the right is another faint outline — that of Smith's Brewery chimney. The road is stone overlaid with hard-packed dirt. And not a shop in sight.

One of the town wells was situated in the road centre between the farm and the Suffolk Place. It was distinguished by having a pine tree north and south of the well itself which survived into the 18th century.

25 Almost unbelievably this photograph, taken about the time that
criminals were still being transported to Botany Bay for their crimes,
shows Sevenoaks High Street at what is now the busiest part of the
modern scene. The nearest building (now part of Hoad's shop) was then
a farrier's forge, complete with hitchpost outside. Next was the
Holmesdale Tavern run by Mr T. Dan, and close by, Amos Pett's basket
shop. At the far end can be seen Bligh's Hotel and brewery.

26 One of the earliest photographs of Sevenoaks High Street — its date
is about 1860 — from an original copied by Essenhigh Corke, later
re-copied by Brunton and then by the author. The street was little but a
dirt track flanked by residences with a few shops between them. In the
absence of traffic wardens, the odd cart driver could park outside the
Holmesdale Tavern while he quenched his thirst at the bar. The Old
Market House can just be seen with the butter market underneath —
open to the four winds. The few street lights consisted of posts and
lanterns supporting colza oil lamps.

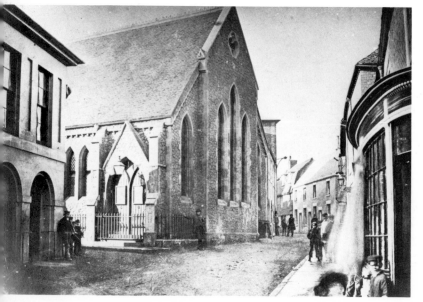

27 A lovely picture from 1880 of the equivalent of today's 'Beeline' taxis. The carriage, one of many in Sevenoaks in the 1860s, may have been part of a commercial venture or, even more likely, belonged to one of the monied families in the town. It is standing outside what is now Woolworth's but, when this picture was made, the shop was a furniture emporium owned by Mr Martin. He later amalgamated with Mr Dolton and the firm of Martin and Dolton came to an end on the death of the latter who ended business as an antique dealer at the beautiful White House, now demolished, at the top of the High Street.

28 Bank Street, Sevenoaks, as it looked some ten years after the advent of the Penny Post. The wooden-ness of the figures shows that the photographer had to give an exceptionally long exposure, everyone standing still while the wet-plate was exposed. They were not able to stop the wind from blowing the awnings on the corner shop, however, which obliterated at least one small boy in all but his legs which can be seen below the blur.

A careful examination will reveal the Inn sign of the Black Boy public house and the absence of our present day shops farther up. Today's café was then a Methodist chapel, and the Old Market House had not yet become a public convenience, the upper part being used for meetings and debates.

29 An extremely rare, unpublished photograph of two of the shops on Sevenoaks High Street. One can only guess at the age but it was probably 1875 or thereabouts when a roving photographer decided that Mr Gandy and Mr Amos Pett should have their respective shops immortalised. Apart from Elliman's Embrocation, Mr Gandy sold brushes, sponges, saddles and tack. He was probably well established by the time Mr Outram came to Sevenoaks and opened up in opposition in 1886.

Amos Pett the basket maker was well known in Sevenoaks. He may have been a descendant of William Pett who was a local benefactor in Tudor times but at any rate, he was active in many local institutions and a keen cricketer to boot. Most local mothers proudly aired their progeny in one of Mr Pett's beautifully made basket-work baby carriages. These two shops were right opposite what is now Woolworth's.

30 Sevenoaks once contained as many public houses and ale bars as it did shops. Many of them are now doing duty as private residences. Among these are the Cats, the Six Bells, the Coachmakers Arms, the Rock and Fountain — while the Royal Oak, the Foresters, the Holmesdale, the Rose and Crown and the Royal Crown have given way to commercial uses. This picture, *circa* 1890, shows, on the left, the Oddfellows and Foresters' Arms which faced the Rose and Crown in Sevenoaks High Street.

On the right can be seen Marchant and Wright's the haberdashers, Pearce's fishmongery and, if we could see round the corner, Whyntie's clothing store. The Old Market House, still with open basement, can just be seen peeping over the Bank Street area.

31 A scene which must be well-remembered to the older members of the present community of Sevenoaks. Sweetly nostalgic too, when one remembers Salmons, where our parents bought us our first toys for a few pence, and, in later life, we bought our tools and domestic bits from Mr Franks, at the shop on the extreme right.

Perhaps the best known shop was Marchant and Wright's, almost obscured by the smaller cart. In this Victorian emporium, no lady could ask in vain for any article of haberdashery. We remember, too, the iron grille in the floor — a trap for high heels — from which heat rose from hot pipes, and the fascinating aerial rail on which travelled little containers holding bills or change, shot by rubber catapults between the sales points and the central cashier. Also on the right, midway, can just be seen the Rose and Crown Hotel which originally took the 'overflow' of stage coach passengers from the Royal Crown.

32 This little building had a history. Alas, it was pulled down only a few years ago after having served as a fruiterer's store shed. In about 1770 John Wesley came to Sevenoaks and preached in the open, near the Grammar School. He was so well received that he returned on many occasions. A shopkeeper, Mrs George, was his chief supporter and made her shop the centre of Methodism in the area. That shop was at 78 High Street (today Barclay's Bank). Eventually the little Methodist chapel was built at the end of Redman's Place and opened by Wesley in 1774. It served for many years but was forsaken when the chapel in Bank Street was opened. Its last use was as a headquarters for the Sevenoaks Liberal Association after which, considerably dilapidated, it was used to store the fruiterer's boxes.

33 One can imagine the frustration of the photographer who took this picture some 100 years ago. With his wet-plate camera, he stood inside a portable darkroom to make his exposure after enjoining everyone in sight to keep still for at least half a minute. Despite his care, the boy between the two bowler hatted men in the foreground has two heads, a shadowy form outside Franks' ironmongery records the passing of a small figure and the boy in the road with two sticks has become blurred by his own movement, slight though it was. The old gentleman on the right is just stepping off after his pause — no doubt exasperated at this pandering to dangerous modern inventions from which no good could come.

This was Sevenoaks High Street, just below the Chequers, before the car, the aeroplane or the telephone.

34 Sevenoaks market place as it appeared in the early part of the present century. Although modest in size it still boasted cattle pens outside the Chequers and a fair sprinkling of stalls nearer the fountain.

35 The time is somewhere in the eighteen-sixties and the place, the Sevenoaks cattle market at the junction of the High Street and London Road. The market had a Charter perhaps granted by the King, although if a charter still exists, it is probably in the Knole archives and relates to a grant made by Archbishop Bourchier in 1463: the author is aware that a deed was found at Knole in 1905 but its subsequent fate is unknown. In 1618 the market rights belonged to the Sackvilles but they took no tolls. And from the turn of the century until recent times, cattle were sold in the streets.

Later the Kent and Sussex Farmers acquired the rights by purchase, and eventually the Urban Council assumed control of them in 1924 under the powers of the Public Health Act, making bye-laws to cover any misuse. There have been squabbles about the matter ever since.

This photograph is a reminder of the days when every local farmer took his cattle to Sevenoaks each Saturday to sell.

36 This was the main post office of Sevenoaks in the year 1890. They were celebrating the jubilee of the establishment of the Penny Post. A letter posted one day would reach its destination in the following day despite the fact that postmen went by foot on their deliveries in the towns and villages of England. The archway in the picture led to the yard at the rear and you can still see today the nameplate in this archway referring to Post Office Yard.

37 King George V, the grandfather of our Queen, was born in 1865, the year this photograph was posed and taken. It shows the busiest part of the High Street where the entrance to the Buckhurst car park now lies. The original was extremely faded but, thanks to the skill of Alex Watson, this photograph still constitutes a significant record of early days in our town. Sevenoaks School boys can be seen in their gowns and mortar-board headgear.

Fifth from the left is a figure, ill-defined, but with a yoke carrying two milk buckets. The two men in uniform look like policemen, but it is almost certain that they were members of the Sevenoaks Volunteer Brigade wearing, if so, the second type of uniform. They were part of the Kent Rifles, 33rd Company, and give the photograph its date.

38 There are many records of the Fountains area of Sevenoaks in existence but this one, taken in the late 19th century, shows the expanse of dirt road which existed before the coming of the fountain towards the end of the century. King George V was about five years old when one of the Corke family removed his lens cap to take this picture. Note the photographer's name on the shopfront of what is now the Midland Bank.

An evocative photograph; the only inhabitants are a small dog and, perhaps, its master, a shadowy figure at the foot of the street lamp nearby. Long gone, these shadows from the past, and yet the outline of the roofs and shops of Sevenoaks seem the same, even after a century of progress. Only the occupants of the buildings have changed—the Bank where Mr Corke once carried out his business, and a travel firm at the premises of Mr Payne the pharmacist.

39 Rayley's Corner (so named after the baker and pastrycook) as it was in the late 19th century. The shop on the corner of Six Bells Lane was, earlier, the Six Bells alehouse. Both pub and lane were named after the casting of the peal of six original bells at St Nicholas' Parish Church. The ladies in the trap, it is said, came from Knole. Were they about to visit Jane Austin, or perhaps a member of the Lambarde family, both of whom lived near here?

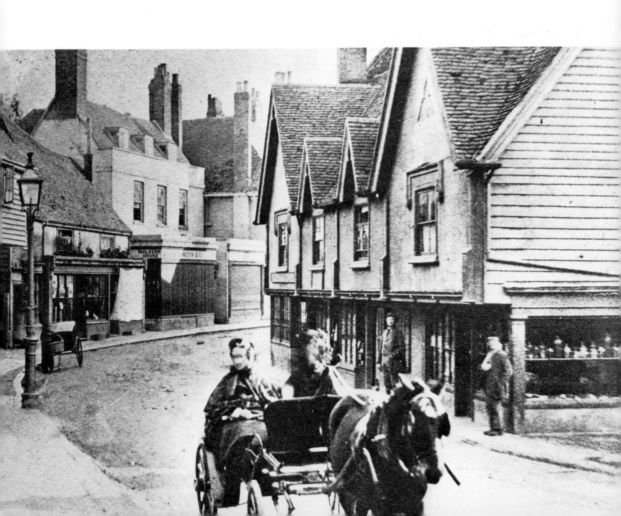

40 An extremely old photograph of Sevenoaks School, the glass negative of which had to be extensively restored, showing the building as it appeared in its early days. The school was founded in 1432. Of the many local benefactors who gave to the school were William Pett, Richard Blackboy and Richard Pett; these three gave some 15 acres of land near the Vine for the use of the school. A poster discovered recently indicates that this land was sold by auction in 1827.

42 The old gym at Sevenoaks School, about 1908. It shows the conventional apparatus which was still in use up to the late twenties. The boys 'frozen' in the photograph must now be in their nineties or no longer with us.

41 A notice advertising the letting of the School lands near the Vine, over a century and a half ago. The notice advertises the land as being suitable for a nursery or market garden: it seems likely that Turner's nurseries were established on part of the land. Who Mr Quait was, or Mr Clout, the printer, is a matter of conjecture, but the odds are that Mr Clout's printing presses were in Old Post Office Yard as I know that a printer had the buildings which are now the garages of the *Sevenoaks Chronicle*.

School Lands,
SEVENOAKS, KENT.

To be Let by Auction,

At the ROYAL OAK INN, SEVENOAKS;

On Thursday, the 21st of September, 1820,

In ONE or MORE LOTS;

(Subject to such Conditions, as shall be then and there produced;)

All those several Pieces or Parcels of Land, commonly called or known by the Name of the

School Lands,

Situate near the VINE, in

Sevenoaks;

and containing altogether, about

14 Acres & Half

With a convenient BARN, &c. thereon,

In a good state of Cultivation, and well calculated for a Nursery or Market Garden.

Further Particulars may be had by applying to Messrs. WILLARD and COLE, Solicitors, Sevenoaks; or to Mr. H. ROSE, of the same Place, Auctioneer.

☞ The Auction will commence precisely at Five o'Clock in the Afternoon.

CLOUT, Printer, Stationer, &c. Sevenoaks.

43 "When all the world was young, lad". The beautiful photograph
calls to mind the era of Grimes and the little boys who were forced to
climb up chimneys to clean them. It was the time when Sevenoaks was a
quiet market town with little to disturb its even tenor other than the
regular arrivals and departures of the stage coaches at the Royal Oak
Hotel seen here, middle right. The pipes on the left are significant. They
were probably to pipe water here for the first time.

The picture is more than a century old, yet it could almost have been
taken last week for this, the area of Sevenoaks School and the Alms
Houses, still adheres to its original outline.

44 Evening draws on and the farmer and his wife of 80 years ago drive
slowly out of Sevenoaks on the road to the Weald. They pass the School
and the Royal Oak Hotel where kings and princes have stayed. On, past
Oak End and Park Grange into the open country beyond. The smoke
from the gatehouse lends a strangely domestic note to the picture taken
about 1880.

Occupations

45 Was a policeman's lot a happy one in 1880? He had no car or radio. In many cases the only method of travel was the bicycle — leaving the police trap as the Sergeant's perk.

This was the Halstead policeman and typical of the police of the Sevenoaks area of a century ago. He walked his beat, used the stick to correct small boys 'summarily', and knew every person in his 'patch', good or bad.

47 Hygiene was not the fetish that it is today when this photograph was taken about 1890. Fish was delivered (as fast as possible) by horse and cart and from any kind of box that was handy. It is fairly obvious that the margarine box in which this fish was being carried fell off the back of the fishmonger's cart and is being hastily retrieved, not without a bit of hilarity. The lane is at Halstead, just below the original Rectory.

46 The dairy man. In his cart he had a large copper-bound churn almost filled to the brim with milk. On a rail fixed inside hung the various stoops with which he would measure and serve the amount wanted by the customer. This man was employed by the Bradbourne Farm Dairy who, in 1912 advertised 'We hope that by prompt and personal attention to business, scrupulous cleanliness and by purveying only an article of a high standard of excellence and purity, to merit the confidence and support of the inhabitants of Sevenoaks.'

48 Despite the fact that, today, we pay heavy rates for street cleaning and what is called amenity cleaning, our highways and byways cannot compare for cleanliness with those of the old Lengthsmen who took an immense pride in their work around the turn of the century. They were responsible for a length of road. Their duties were to keep that length clean, tidy and safe for the people who used it. They had their own tools and handcart and apart from cleaning they were also responsible for mending and maintenance of road and footpath. They even kept the grass verges cut and trimmed. This man, photographed in Halstead parish, lived and worked there all his life.

49 Mr. Atkins of the Sevenoaks G.P.O., who for about 40 years, delivered the mail from Sevenoaks to the outlying areas, principally those of Halstead, Knockholt and Downe. He was especially proud of his horses and timekeeping. It is said that clocks could be checked by the time of his arrival at any particular place on his route. His stables were behind the Royal Crown Hotel at Sevenoaks.

50 There are still many people who remember the imposing gentleman at the right of this photograph, taken just before the first world war.

He was 'Doctor' Sequar, an itinerant and, almost certainly, unqualified practitioner who, when not selling patent medicines, posed as a chiropodist or even a dentist. He was seen at Sevenoaks market place and other town fairs all over the South of England. Here he is carrying out repairs to a customer's foot. The expressions of those watching tell their own story.

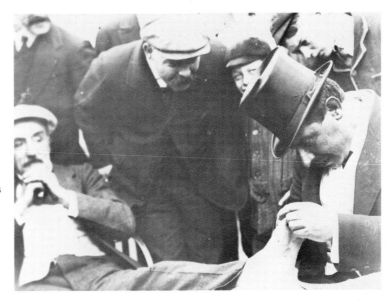

51 There was a time when Gipsies were skilled at basket work and rural crafts, unlike those of today whose principal occupation is the recovery of metal. More often than not, in the 1800s, gipsies were handsome, swarthy and proud descendants of true Romanies. This photograph was of a family called Pettigrove who regularly toured the Sevenoaks area.

52 This picture reflects the poverty which existed in our area in the early part of this century. Eminently respectable families had to undertake most menial tasks in order to make ends meet. The photograph, taken at the Sevenoaks Gas Works yard, shows women helping pick coke and grade it. They were paid 1½d an hour for this never-ending task.

53 The countryman's greatest enjoyment was to shoot over rough countryside and many of those in Sevenoaks extended facilities for shooting parties.

This photograph, taken about 1900, shows a local party containing the brothers Blundell of Halstead. The importance of the picture is that the Falstaffian gentleman third from the left is none other than W. G. Grace, the man who dominated British cricket for over 40 years. In first class cricket he scored 54,896 runs including 126 centuries and took 2876 wickets. On three occasions he made more than 300 runs in an innings. Grace was a frequent visitor to Halstead Place. He died about five years after this photograph was taken.

54 One of the most important of the many rural industries in the Sevenoaks area was the manufacture of charcoal — charred oak wood being reduced to carbon by a controlled burning lasting several days. The product has many uses but particularly in the manufacture of gunpowder, filters and for burning, with draught, to produce great temperatures. This photograph was taken by the author at Pilot Wood, Shoreham.

55 Sevenoaks was in the forefront when it came to fire fighting. The Town had a fine volunteer brigade. It was established in 1820 by the Board of Guardians and used the same fire engine until January 3, 1883 when a new 'Ready' fire engine was bought by public subscription. The town was decorated on the occasion of its delivery. It was drawn by four horses up Tub's Hill with the men of the brigade riding on it and escorted by the Tonbridge Town Band. At the fountain the engine was christened 'Ready' by the little daughter of the captain, Mr. Stepney. A dinner was held that evening to mark the important occasion. Four years later the Brigade managed to quell the great Knole fire, using this engine to do it.

. . . It was also this engine that was instrumental in quelling the blaze at Mr. Essenhigh-Corke's photographic studio. The brigade was taken over, arbitrarily, by the Urban Council, a paltry £50 paid for the engine which was then worth more than £200. The Volunteers were Capt. W. Stepney, H. Pett, G. Stokes, T. Porter, A. Baker, G. Langridge, H. Bartholomew, H. Townsend, E. Tye, H. Tootell, E. Bevan and C. Card.

This photograph shows the Volunteer brigade outside Montreal House, Riverhead.

56 Of all the sweet shops in Sevenoaks there were two which will be especially remembered by the boys of Sevenoaks School. One was (and is) the tuckshop at the High Street post office immediately opposite the school and the other (now a coffee house) was Bert Budgen's little emporium opposite Six Bells Lane. Bert was wise in the ways of small boys and few ever successfully took a rise out of him. A very kindly man, he was an expert furniture repairer who chose the less skilled business of serving in his general store. He was there for some 50 years.

57 There were hundreds of bakers in the Sevenoaks district, but none so well known as Mr. A. Cecil Brown, whose bakery in the old Bligh's brewery building supplied cakes, pastries and bread for the shop in London Road. Mr. Brown, who at one time was President of the Master Bakers' Association, was also celebrated as a billiards player. He was Secretary of the Cornwall Men's Club for 53 years. The walls of the club are decorated with several certificates of the British Billiards Association for his making 100 breaks.

58 A photograph by Alex Watson of one of the best known piano tuners in the Sevenoaks area. He was Mr. Percy Lewis who, with his wife, had the shop in Bank Street originally run by Traylen and Phillips. There they sold phonographs, gramophones, sheet music, violins, autoharps and mouth organs. Mr. Lewis was blind and was trained by St. Dunstans in piano tuning. Sadly, Mrs. Lewis became blind also, and the couple had to sell the business, retaining only the tuning of pianos which Mr. Lewis continued to his death in 1978. Even blind, he was able to repair, restring and on one occasion, re-design a piano. In this picture he is seen French Polishing a piano case.

59 Chapters could be written about this man, Mr. Frank Bond of Knockholt. He was born about 1890 when there seemed to be a fresh invention of import every day. Frank Bond was one of those men who, with an affinity for engineering, had to involve himself in mechanics, electricity, motoring and in anything new and exciting. He was a cyclist of some fame who regularly won the Westerham hill climb. He had the first motor cycle in Knockholt and the first motor car. He experimented with telephones and wireless, had an electrically driven workshop before most engineers in London. He ran a taxi business and coal business. His greatest hobby and pursuit was the making of organs. The inventor of the 'Bondmag' — an electric method of actuating organ pipes — he made his own three manual organ in a shed at home, completely filling the shed. Many local churches still have organs made by him.

60 The porter at Dunton Green station is not handing the engine driver a Leica camera on its strap. It was a far more important instrument, one absolutely vital to any trip on the branch line between Dunton Green and Westerham. The object was the tablet without which no journey on the line was possible. It was handed to the signalman who inserted the tablet into a control which allowed him to drop the signal for the journey. The tablet would then be handed to the driver who, at the completion of his journey, would adopt the same method with the Westerham signalman. Thus two trains could never be on the single track at the one time.

61 As is today, every section of every railway in the country is controlled by signalmen who operate the signals along the lines. This picture, taken by the author in 1931 at Dunton Green box, illustrates the physical aspect of signal control in those days. Each semaphore type signal had to be raised or lowered by cables between them and the signal box. Considerable effort was involved in operating a 'distant' signal. Today signals are operated by electricity and small toggle switches.

62 Every village had its own farrier in the days when travel was by horse or horse-drawn vehicle. In Sevenoaks there were several such men who could shoe a horse in less than half an hour. One was George Terry, whose forge in Old Post Office Yard is still carried on by Mr W. Pearce. George was one of the Sevenoaks Firemen for many years. In this photograph, taken by the author in 1948, he is seen drawing a shoe from the fire before giving it the final shape on the anvil.

Transport

63 The old Sevenoaks 'Ready' fire engine which helped to quell the Knole fire of 1887 *(see Nos.74 & 75)*. It was discovered by the author in a barn at Salter's Heath where it had lain, under straw and debris, for forty years. It may have been bought by the farmer for irrigation purposes and was in good condition when found. The pump was operated by men, eight a side. The hoses were leather.

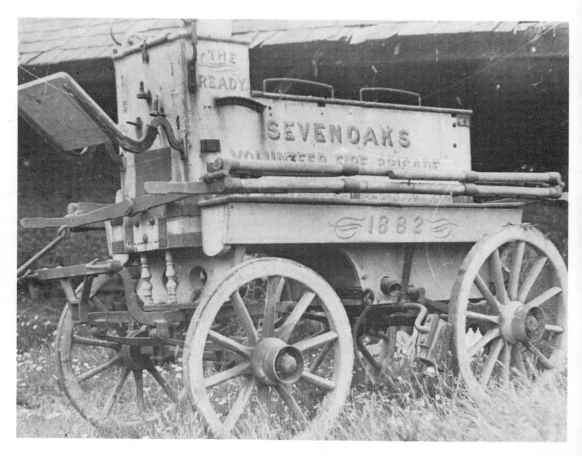

64 Sevenoaks traders, like those in any other part of the country around the turn of the century, took an immense pride in their delivery vans and horses. They had regular concourses d'elegance on Knole Paddock and proudly carried the rosettes on their horses' harness. This delivery cart, Number 3 in the fleet, was part of the stable of Uridge the grocer.

65 When Boots' chemists shop was in the market place of Sevenoaks, opposite the Chequers, and the Sevenoaks Gas Company's offices were next door, much of the traffic was horse-drawn. This photograph is of one of the wagons from a Sevenoaks Weald farm which delivered hay bales to local corn merchants.

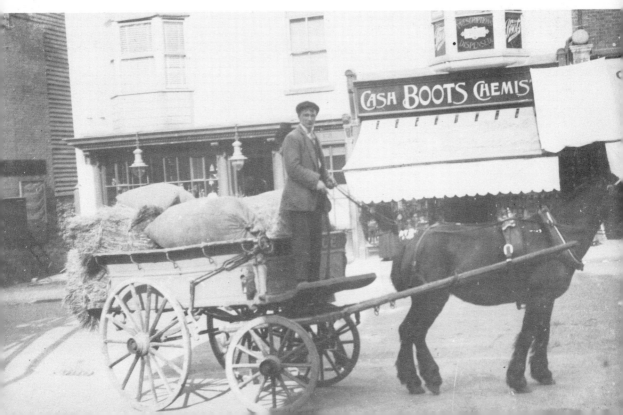

66 An early photograph, about 1907, showing the manner in which the produce from Sevenoaks farms was taken to Covent Garden market each day. The cart, from Blundell's farm, Shoreham, would carry 120 bushel baskets full of farm produce. The horse did the double journey to and from London without fatigue. If the driver happened to be tired, and 'dropped off' to sleep, the horse would take him home regardless, knowing the route as well as his human companion.

67 A shocking rail tragedy which occcurred in Sevenoaks station on June 7 1884 as the double headed goods train from Deal ran into the rear of another goods train after an error in 'block working', a signal technique. The crash, at 25 miles an hour, resulted in the complete wrecking of two engines and several trucks which were scattered over a wide area. The driver and fireman of the pilot loco were both killed but, despite the second engine having rolled completely over, the driver and fireman of this were unscathed.

68 This was one of the unusual machines which carried passengers on the Westerham branch line. It once carried Sir Winston Churchill. It was a Sentinel railcar with controls at either end, obviating the necessity to change locos. The photograph was taken in 1936.

69 An early picture of Westerham station on the branch line from Dunton Green, taken about 1904 when the line was being used regularly. There was a time when the railway was scheduled to continue to Oxted and cuttings were already effected but had to be abandoned as part of a 'deal' by the South Eastern Railway company. The branch was officially opened in July 1881. It was closed on October 28, 1961 as supposedly uneconomic. The author was on the last train to run over the Westerham rails. A few days earlier, he filmed a complete run from the air — from Westerham to Dunton Green.

70 The 'mashers' of the 1900s, awheel and fancy free. These were the gentlemen of the cycling clubs which sprang up following the perfection of the pedal cycle.

This photograph, taken by one of the members of the club pictured, was posed outside the Amherst Arms Hotel, Riverhead. The pub was then a Cyclists Touring Club headquarters catering especially for cyclists. The gentleman in the foreground was the proud owner of the latest tricycle.

71 Quinnell & Sons, furniture removers, of Bradbourne Road, Sevenoaks, were established in 1814. Years ago they dealt in coal and coke supplies. Later there was a fruit and vegetable shop too.

This picture, taken about 1880, shows part of the large fleet of extremely costly steam traction engines and delivery furniture vans. Notice that there is not a rubber tyre in sight. The photo was taken at Riverhead, where Bradbourne Vale Road joins the London Road.

72 Dunton Green has long been the home of local buses. In the late twenties the garage was built at the foot of Barrett's Road to contain the fleet and to provide a place for maintenance. The East Surrey Traction Company started the fleet which was later absorbed by London Transport. Today it is run by London Country Bus Services. Originally open top B. type buses were used, two of which can be seen in this photograph.

73 When the East Surrey Traction Co. was building up its fleet for local bus services between Sevenoaks and Farnborough, most of the stock was parked in the open in Barrett's Road, Dunton Green, on the site of what later became the garage shown above. In the interim, they borrowed the yard at the Railway Tavern for carrying out engine changes and repairs. The union wouldn't have approved of the conditions there: look at the few paltry tarpaulins for working cover.

Great Houses

74 & 75   The people of Sevenoaks today are probably unaware that
Knole House was only saved from destruction by a group of volunteer
firemen with a hand-operated water pump. The potentially disastrous fire
occurred in 1887 when 300 tons of hay in the side barn caught alight.
The alarm was given by the Rector of Seal who, seeing smoke issuing in
great volumes, whipped up his horses and tore to the fire station.
Fireman Pett, who was already dressed, joined other firemen on their
curricle engine and drove to Knole where the fire blazed.

   The Volunteer brigade was already there with the town 'Ready' engine
and between them they held the fire away from the main house, and
finally brought it under control. There is no doubt that Sevenoaks' main
attraction would have been lost had it not been for these men and their
prompt action.

76 At the time of the accession of Queen Victoria, Beechmont, situated on the ridge above Sevenoaks Weald, was owned by the Lambarde family. It was destroyed in 1945 by a 'doodle-bug'.

I have a dozen or more photographs of this rambling old house but this one is exceptional because it contains one of the Boxhill to London stage coaches and also Gore Lambarde, the then owner of the house. He was a man who delighted in horse-drawn vehicles, particularly fours-in hand, and it is he who appears in the 'driving seat' of the coach which, no doubt, like the Duke of Edinburgh, he took for an airing on occasions.

77 Bradbourne, and the famous Bradbourne Bell. This ancient pile was one of the stately homes which influenced Sevenoaks in no small degree. Syd Bishop, the demolisher bought it in the end, but it had been the home of the Bosvilles from 1555 to 1760, of Sir Richard Betenson and his relatives to about 1840 and, among others, of Mr. Francis Crawshay, an adept in Druidism who 'planted' the various stones and monoliths, some of which still survive. The Lambardes were the last owners.

78 Go down Mill Lane, at Greatness, and on your right will be the little Scout hut which belongs to the St. Johns' troop. It was on this spot that the great house of the Nouaille family — Greatnesse — originally stood, close by the silk mills which the family operated. When they ceased in business the house was sold to the Filmer family.

It eventually became semi-derelict and, about the time of the first world war, was bought by a film company who blew it up as 'realism' in a war film.

79 Montreal, at Riverhead, as it appeared more than a century ago. It was built by Jeffery Amherst in 1764 from stones of a previous home called Brooks. Amherst created the park of Montreal and erected a fine monolith to commemorate the meeting of the three Amherst brothers after the surrender of Canada. The monolith still stands.

A peculiarity of this photograph is the likeness of a poodle formed on the wall of Montreal by the growth of ivy.

80 A particularly fine photograph of Chipstead Place which, during the first world war, was converted into a hospital to which many wounded Belgian soldiers were brought from the battlefields of Flanders. It was to this hospital that a Belgian woman made her way in a desperate attempt to find her husband. She managed to pass through the German lines to the coast, received a free passage from the captain of a Merchant Navy vessel and, without a word of English, found her way to Chipstead where she was re-united with her husband. The story was in almost every publication in England.

Special Occasions

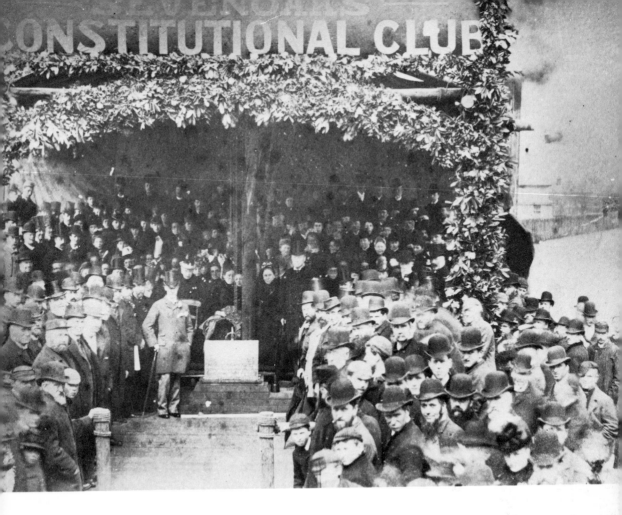

81 This captivating photograph, taken at the Polhill Arms around 1880, marks a special excursion for a party of almost 80 people.

Clearly this was a 'stag' party, perhaps on an outing from London — maybe the equivalent of our present day 'darts team' visit to a neighbouring county.

Whatever it was, it was sufficiently important to warrant the use of no less than four stage coaches with men in livery. Over the heads of the two horses at the extreme right can be seen the tonneau of a car, halted until such time as the photographer had done his work.

82 This is probably the only photograph in existence of a stage-coach at work in Sevenoaks. Although it is of a genuine coach which once plied between London and the coast, it was bought by the proprietor of the Royal Oak Hotel as a memento of earlier times. This photograph was taken, about 1880, to mark its last journey. In 1803 such coaches drove, daily, with mail for Sevenoaks from the Nag's Head, or the Talbot, Southwark, depots of Mr Longford and Mr Sulby — carriers.

83 Hard hats were the order when the Constitutional Club foundation stone was laid, not in the north east corner but at the south end of the building. The year was 1889; the site between the Dartford Road and Seal Hollow. The building was raised by the Constitutional Club Company for social and political meetings and contained billiards, smoking and committee rooms, refreshment bar and cloakrooms. The Club Hall adjoined on the north side. It is said that two new sovereigns were placed under the stone. Presumably these were recovered when the building was later adapted as offices for Messrs Vallis and Struthers, solicitors.

84 Sevenoaks has always had a hard core of literary and theatrical societies. This photograph, taken in the first decade of this century, is of the members of the Sevenoaks Literary, Scientific and Debating Society. Their original headquarters were the rooms over the Old Market House. Here, Lord Sackville gave a lecture on the sport of yachting and Violet Sackville West one on Knole; Col. Schwartz spoke on Egyptology and Col. Fisher on explosives. The members kept abreast of scientific discoveries of the times.

85 This photograph illustrates one of the lesser mysteries of 19th century Sevenoaks. On February 18th, 1894 a disastrous fire broke out at Mr Dray's shop, situated just below Horncastle's in the High Street. Despite the urgent attention of the Sevenoaks Ready Brigade, the premises were severely damaged. The firemen saved a good portion of the building, however, and a large percentage of stock. The Chief of the Brigade was worried about the origin of the fire but nothing was said publicly.

When a second and even more disastrous fire broke out in Mr Dray's shop on March 29th, destroying what was left of the stock (happily well insured), Sevenoaks began talking. It is said, though there is no confirmation, that Mr Dray was eventually prosecuted in connection with the fires. This photograph shows members of the Brigade posing with a policeman in front of the gutted premises. The man with the beard is almost certainly Fireman E. Tye, the engineer who later became Fire Chief.

Fire at Mr Drews

86 Ballooning was the particular interest of the adventurous in the 19th century, and although there is a complete record of an ascent at Seal in 1825 by Mr A. Peal, most of the recorded ascents from Sevenoaks were about the turn of the century from the top of the slope at Knole Paddock where a gas main had been installed by the Sevenoaks Gas Company for the purpose of inflating the huge envelopes. Principal balloonist was Captain Percival Spencer whose balloons Vivienne 1, 2 and 3 were often to be seen in Sevenoaks. The author's father, as a young man, went up with Spencer and despite a rough ride was captivated by the experience. This picture was taken at Knole Paddock in 1901. There were other local balloonists, such as Mr C. Bucknell and the then occupant of Wickhurst Manor.

87 In April 1901 arrangements for the Coronation of Edward VII were well in hand. It was something of a shock when, just after a public meeting in the Club Hall to finalise the arrangements, news came that the King was ill. On June 26th, the day before the Coronation, news came that the event was to be postponed indefinitely. Sevenoaks decided to go ahead with its arrangements. Despite heavy thunderstorms on the 30th a massive Coronation bonfire was ignited in Bligh's Meadow. A dinner for the Active service men was given at the Drill Hall by Capt. J.D. Laurie. The St John's Church Lads Brigade were reviewed by the Prince of Wales and Lord Roberts.

On July 9th, a Coronation dinner was given at the Drill Hall for all Sevenoaks residents over 50 years of age, and on Dukes' Meadow the Coronation sports for the children was washed out by a particularly heavy storm. The same applied the the Coronation tea on the Vine. On August 9th (Coronation Day) everyone over 60 was invited to a dinner in the Drill Hall and, as this photograph shows, more than 400 people attended.

88 Sevenoaks High Street in the days of the Great War. This is from a faded box Brownie photograph of about 1915 and shows two Gunners driving a field gun and limber in the direction of Tonbridge. They have just passed the Chequers in the High Street and are approaching the old Dairy which is now the Midland Bank. We can just make out the name of J. Westall whose hairdressing salon backed on to the dairy premises.

89 No book of this kind would be complete without at least one photograph of the Home Guard of the Second World War. This shows units returning from a drumhead service and march-past at the Vine on June 4th 1944 in 'Salute the Soldier' week. The Company D. had its farewell dinner on December 1st, 1944 at Knole Golf Club.

There is one story about this unit which bears repetition. There was a spigot mortar competition at Panthurst Farm Weald on October 24th, 1943. The driver of the van which was to take the 'ammo' down to the farm was about to move off when one of the H.G. passengers nervously asked if the ammo was 'live'. When told that it was, he was of the opinion that it was 'a bit dangerous'. When assured by the driver that it would probably be all right, he hopped out, put on his steel helmet, returned to sit on the ammo box with equanimity, and a self-satisfied smile. The picture shows No.6 Platoon, 'A' Company, Captain Oliver in command.

90 This plywood black-out board has become famous, because the scrawled signatures are the names of the Battle of Britain pilots who flew during the war from Biggin Hill. They chalked their names on the board which covered one of the windows of the White Hart pub in Brasted. It was carefully saved, framed and mounted in a place of honour in the pub until, some 28 years later, it was acquired by the R.A.F. for their museum at Hendon. 'Sailor' Malan's signature is here, along with those of Brian Kingcome, Sqdn. Ldr. Tuck, Johnny London, 'Al' Deer, Neville Duke, Wing Cdr. Brothers and a score of other well known Battle of Britain names.

91 Regulations and the lack of materials made photographs of Sevenoaks during the war few and far between. This photograph is reproduced from the *Sevenoaks Chronicle* of 1939. It was taken on the 'down' platform of Sevenoaks station as the first load of refugee children from London arrived to be billeted with local families for the duration. Within a year or so, most of these children had returned to their homes, convinced that Sevenoaks was quite as dangerous as London. When, later, the Flying Bombs came, Sevenoaks certainly *was* dangerous. But by that time there was hardly a refugee child in the district.

92 No wonder Seal Hollow Road and Dartford Road were both blocked by people on this special occasion just after the '39-'45 War. A glance at the window of the Constitutional Club reveals the reason. Sir Winston Churchill had come to Sevenoaks to boost support for the new Member — John Rodgers. Conservative Sevenoaks turned out as never before, if only to see, at close range, the man who had led this country to Victory.

93 History books record that, on Sevenoaks Common, seven oak trees have stood since time immemorial and that, from one such group, the town derived its name. A few years ago (about 1960) the seven trees that have continued this tradition for more than a century, were felled by Peter Smith of the Invicta Company, for the Urban District Council. The councillors held that they were diseased but when felled they proved to be of sound substance. Seven new oaks were planted to continue the tradition. All but one have survived and that one continues to be replaced until, finally, it takes root with the others.

Weald

94   An extremely old photograph (about 1868) of Sevenoaks Weald showing the road from the village looking towards the church in the distance below. The road, now a well-used highway, was at this time nothing more than a dirt track.

95 Few old photographic records of Sevenoaks Weald seem to have survived, but this, of the village church, has reached us in fine condition. It appears to have been taken late in the last century and poses a small problem. The tower looks squat and may have been slightly altered in more recent years. The author was assured, by the owner of the original, that the large, bushy tree on the left of the churchyard was a haunted spot, and that several local people had been recorded as having seen the unmistakably ghostly figure of a young woman coming out from this spot, or disappearing into it. The legend is an old one.

96 This beautiful Kentish windmill stood the four winds for more than 100 years. It stood at Watts Cross below Sevenoaks Weald and on the main road to Hildenborough. It was demolished only twenty years or so ago after having become too derelict in the war years to be repaired.

Seal

97 There could be no more poignant contrast with present-day Seal than this photograph of the village taken a century ago. The A25 today is so crammed with traffic that the pedestrian is hard put to cross from one side to the other which tends to make Seal a village divided. This scene shows a peaceful calm of days long gone. On the right was the forge and the tree which stood outside. It seems to have rained, for the road is deeply marked with ruts and the only vehicles on the road are two carts, and even those are without their horses.

98 This photograph was almost certainly taken at the same time as the previous one looking towards Sevenoaks. This time the photographer is facing along the same A25 towards Ightham. The Kentish Yeoman figures in this picture, the Crown in the one above.

99 An intriguing photograph of Church Road, Seal. Judging from the clues it was taken about 1903, or 1905. One clue is the knickerbocker fashion, as used by the youth on the left. The other is the box camera he is holding. It was a type which used glass plates, and these were changed by dropping them, with a small lever on top of the camera, into a 'reservoir' at the bottom of the camera.

It is difficult to remember the last time anyone saw cows making their way from the High Street down this lane. Almost certainly they were going to the farm by Seal Church to be milked. What a delight if somebody recognised the people in the photograph.

100 To my mind reminiscent of the infamous Paris tumbrils which took the aristocrats to the guillotine, this fearsome looking vehicle was probably the last word in comfort and excitement to the small boys and girls who rode in it, before the First World War. They are about to leave Seal, by the Crown Inn, for some unknown destination, probably a summer camp. The Scouts seem to have been given the forward seats and the Guides those at the back. A slight touch of chauvinism, perhaps.

101 St Edith's Well, Kemsing, is now one of the local beauty spots where an annual pilgrimage is held. When this photo was taken, more than 100 years ago, it could hardly have been so described. In those days, any well was an important village object, used by almost everybody. Often a village well, like this one, was the only place where water could be obtained unless one had a private well. The young lady leaning on the wall has her two pails which were attached, for the journey to and from the well, to a yoke which sat comfortably on her shoulders. It is interesting to note the little stream rising from the ground on the left and running at the back of the well.

Otford & Shoreham

102 A rare photograph of the paper mill which thrived on the water of the Darent at Shoreham. Apparently this river had particular properties which were essential in the making of paper. Here, high grade writing paper and a superior grade of cartridge were produced by local labour. At Eynsford, only a few miles away, and at Sundridge, paper was produced for British bank notes.

103 Twitton about 1878, when this photograph was taken, was composed of some eight or nine cottages, a farm with oasts, and a pub, the Rising Sun. Between these ran a small dirt track leading to Danesfield and the Shoreham to Polhill road. This is one of the only really old photo-records of this village to have survived.

104 Shoreham, one of the most beautiful of the villages in the Sevenoaks area, still attracts thousands of visitors in the summer months. This photograph, taken about 1908, emphasises the fact that no piped water was available at the time. The small boy carrying water with the aid of a yoke had obviously been to the Darent for supplies for his parents in the cottages near the Church. No doubt, in his spare time, he fished in the river for the trout which abounded there.

105 Otford, being a naturally beautiful village, has had the attention of photographers for more than a century. This incredible photo, made on a large glass negative in my possession, shows the village as no other photo has done. The dirt road, rutted and flanked by the stream running from the pond down to the Darent, the cottages and Forge, old even when this picture was taken, the children in rags and the evidence on the road of the passing of many horses, all go to make this a unique record of Otford village.

106 A 'close-up' of the old forge at Otford and the Bull inn opposite. The stream which trickled down to the Darent apparently surfaced here and the miniature bridges at the entrance to each dwelling can plainly be seen. Here, too, there is no line of demarcation between road and footpath.

108 Of the thirty or so old photographs of Otford in my collection this is the one I value most. It was taken, about 1865, where the Darent is crossed by the bridge near Broughton Manor. In my mind I have christened this beautiful and artistic study 'The Gleaners'.

107 Another beautiful photo of Otford from the 19th century, taken in the evening when the cattle were returning from the fields. In the distance, smoke from a chimney drifts across toward the recreation ground of today, then a pasture. The Forge and its cottage, now a restaurant, and the nearer dwellings, now modern shops, are all part of a rural village. The only thing separating footpath from road is a growth of grass and a line of stones.

109 Otford possesses many old and beautiful buildings. This is Pickmoss which stands at the west end of the High Street just before the Darent bridge. The house is probably of 14th or 15th century origin but despite Tudor influence, much of it is modern. This photograph is probably 110 years old. It shows quite plainly that, at one time, a stream flowed the length of the village. On the left can be seen the cottages which were turned into a pub which is still a popular 'local': The Horns.

110 Otford pond, beautiful centrepiece of the village, which has been further enhanced in more recent years. The Otford Preservation Society has contributed more to this area than anyone in the past. This photograph is difficult to date but was probably taken about 1907.

111 An unusual record, and one which, until now, has never been seen. It shows the Otford war memorial, ready for unveiling about 1919. It bore the names of 27 men from the village killed in action. To these were added the names of 7 killed during the 1939-45 war. Otford was divided by a row about money collected to provide a memorial after the first war. Half the village wanted a memorial hall while the Vicar and other members of the church were in favour of a lych-gate. The hall won.

Knockholt & Halstead

112   There seems to be a charm about a genuine folly that attracts many Englishmen. The folly at Knockholt is no exception. Knockholt House was, in 1838, the seat of Joseph Skerritt Esq, Lt. Col. of the 35th Rgt. It was only a short distance from the Church and possessed beautiful gardens overlooking the scarp towards Westerham. James Vavasseur, a wealthy silk merchant, occupied it from 1870 and it was he who completely re-designed the house, providing it with a revolutionary system of heating which used a tall tower to support the chimney. The tower had another significance because Vavasseur, it is firmly held, was convinced that there would be another Biblical deluge, and he wanted to be prepared for it. He had a boat in the tower against the cataclysm which never came. The last resident was Miss C. Vavasseur. When she left it, the house remained empty for a time and was then destroyed.

The photograph, taken about 1900, gives a good idea of the magnificence of the House and the open stairway to the tower which Vavasseur regularly used as an observatory.

113 This charming little cameo was taken in the early part of this century on the lane between what was then called the Oak hotel, and Stoneings farm — probably the oldest in the district. The lady driving the pony and trap lived at one of the topmost homes in Knockholt, by Scott's Corner. For many years she and her family drove such vehicles round the area. Stoneings Farm is now owned by Miss Winnie Constable, of the family of the famous painter. She is compiling a history of her village.

114 Steamrollers, though otherwise almost foolproof, often came to grief when drivers attempted to 'change gear' while the machine was moving. The result was that the engine suddenly gained speed on a slope, the driver had no chance of catching the gears, and disaster followed. An engine's brakes were the steam in the cylinders, apart from a hand operated 'parking' brake which took a long time to apply. This poor victim of its driver's carelessness snapped in two and overturned when it got away on a slight slope at Knockholt and the driver tried to slow it by mounting the kerb.

115 This cottage shop in Old London Road, Knockholt, later a hairdresser's and now a private house, had a draper's business when this photograph was taken in about 1910. A well-dressed trader is apparently leaving to deliver his customers' purchases.

Prior to the cutting of Polhill in 1757 this was one of the most important roads in the district. The London stage coaches stopped at the Harrow Inn just a couple of hundred yards up the road. Almost at this very spot a highwayman held up a stage coach; he was caught, taken to Bromley jail and eventually hanged.

116 This scene from the 'good olde days' was photographed in the very early years of the present century.

Taken at the Halstead Crossroads by what was then the village Post Office, it shows the stage which ran daily between Knockholt Beeches and Knockholt railway station, about three miles away. It is interesting to note the wicker 'holster' in which the coach horn was secured when not in use.

117 Otford Road, Halstead about 1880, when it was little more than a dirt track between the village crossroads and Polhill, used mainly by carts and other horse-drawn vehicles serving the local farms. There is a small mystery in the pub sign of the Royal Crown, then run by Mr Thompson. The sign contains two symbols which have connotations of Freemasonry. As there is no record of a lodge at this hostelry it seems that the landlord may have been a Freemason and was anxious to advertise the fact for the benefit of other masons who might have been passing.

118 If you had been the photographer who took this picture, you could have popped into the pub afterwards and bought a pint of the best beer for only 1½d. At that time a firkin (9 gallons) of beer cost only 12s (60 pence).

The pub was and is, of course, Halstead's Cock Inn, still giving a warm welcome to locals and travellers alike. It stands on the junction of the roads to Knockholt station and Badger's Mount roundabout.

119 Here is a little bit of 'modern' history: Halstead people, queueing at Blundell's farm during the last war, for potatoes. There are at least fifty people visible in the 'crocodile' and there might easily have been a similar number behind them. It is typical of the times that, despite the exhausting business of queueing for long periods for their food, people invariably took the matter as 'part of the day's work'. Most of the people in this photo have smiles on their faces.

120 Approaching Deerleap on the road from Halstead to Knockholt; this photograph was taken, not a century ago, but by the author just after the second war. The car in the distance gives the game away. Mr Ward, the farmer, used the haycart for many years after this picture was taken.

Dunton Green

121 Things got so bad in Dunton Green in the early part of the century that motor cars were burning through at speeds up to 25 miles an hour, to the peril of everyone in the village. Then a little girl was knocked down and killed and, at the inquest, it was actually alleged that the car must have been doing over 25 miles an hour. Following this, the whole village turned out in a mass protest. This part of the procession carried a banner which read 'Please don't kill us.' Another said 'To motorists, Hail. To road-hogs, Hades.' Others read 'Motorists, Live and Let Live' or 'The Police, do your duty.' From that time onward, more motorists were speed-trapped in Dunton Green than anywhere else in the area.

122 The centre of Dunton Green village at the break of this century. The Duke's Head, right, was where the horse peddlars held unofficial sales, trotting their animals round the area of the tree which was not sawn down until the late twenties. In its bole were thirteen different hooks to which horses were tethered in the previous century. Some of these were completely buried in bark and wood, evidence of the growth and age of the tree.

Joey Martin's store was the 'supermarket' of the age. Inside, children spent their Saturday Penny on sweets, Mr Martin weighing them in a pair of balances which pulled down over the counter on a counterbalance. Mr Frayne's Post Office was on the left. The sign can just be seen in this photograph.

123   Longford Mill as it appeared in 1860, with not another building in sight. The Darent can be seen meandering away towards the 'floats' between Dunton Green and Chipstead, where 'nude' bathing was the rule, gentlemen only. On the left are the pastures, often waterlogged from the Long Ford, on which the Marley complex was built. Pastures were also on the east side of Longford Hill and up the slopes to where the railway eventually came.

124   The River Darent had no little influence on Dunton Green. It ran the Mill, watered the roads between the village and Riverhead, and provided a playground for young and old. Once, before it was polluted, it was a trout river. It was also a boating river and, at the 'floats', was deep enough for diving and swimming. For some obscure reason nobody used a swimsuit at the floats, preferring to swim naked, even the son of the local millionaire. Part of the Floats was named 'Tommy Alberts' after a boy who was drowned after being caught in the weed which flourished at that particular spot.

This picture is from an original by Mr Killick of Longford Mill.

125   Those who have wined and dined at Donnington Manor, now the Emma Hotel, at Dunton Green could not fail to be impressed by the beauty of the interior of the 'Tudor' part of the Hotel. It would be a great surprise to some to know that this photograph is of the two cottages which stood on the spot until after the Second World War. The 'manor' was the creation of a local man, Bill Newman, who was an expert in building mock Tudor buildings from materials which were collected from all over the country.

He also built the Grasshopper Inn at Moorhouse (see picture **160**), starting with a tiny building similar to the cottage in this photograph, taken by the author in about 1933.

126 Dunton Green lido, one of the most popular swimming pools in the Sevenoaks area. Built and run by Mr Killick, the pool proved to be an attraction to families from a wide area, even from South London. Teas were served on the wide lawns while small boats were hired out to people who rowed them up the Darent above the pool. The Lido disappeared when the Walter Smith company bought the water rights from Mr Killick and that part of the Darent disappeared into Walter Smith's new lake.

127 Upper Dunton Green where the roads from Polhill and Star Hill join to form the main road through the village. The Rose and Crown pub, to the left of the photograph, was a farmhouse in 1479 called Darkynghole. At the time of this photograph, about 1930, a massive tree, completely hollow, flourished outside the pub on a triangular green. On that green, just after the First War, a large trench mortar, captured from the Germans, stood in the corner by the lamp standard to mark the British victory of 1918. It disappeared so silently one day that few people even noticed it had gone.

128 This old pub in Rye Lane, Dunton Green, was a relic of the days when Welsh miners were cutting the Polhill and Sevenoaks railway tunnels. Called the Railway Tavern, it was on the edge of the Brickworks pond. Years after it had ceased to be a pub, the old 'slate' was discovered, on which the miners notched their debts for drinks, the score being settled every pay-day. The building was last occupied by 'Trigger' Turton, an eccentric horticulturalist, formerly a maths lecturer at London University. The trigger came from trigonometry. The spot now serves the West Kent Cold Storage Co. as a car park, the rest of the company's complex covering the pond area.

129 Looking at this delightful photograph, who would believe that it is a picture of Polhill? The photograph was taken about 1908.

When Polhill was originally cut in the 1750s several skeletons were discovered where the new hill crossed the part of the Pilgrim's Way leading from Chevening to Otford. Some 230 years later the crossroads were again altered when the Sevenoaks by-pass was built. This time I was on the spot and, sure enough, discovered eight more skeletons. As the process of recovery was likely to take more time than the authorities would allow, a 'rescue team' of archaeologists from Maidstone Museum, headed by Mr Brian Philps, took over the dig. They found, as well as this casual burial ground, a Saxon graveyard. The many finds are now in the County Museum.

Riverhead

130 The flow of traffic in 1880 was not quite so important as it is today. In this photograph of Riverhead, at the foot of Amherst Hill, one can quite plainly see the 'law cart' applying a right-hand rule of the road, perhaps to keep an eye on the boys from the village school. A butcher's cart with its deliveryman along with other local 'worthies' can be seen outside the Amherst Arms Hotel — then one of the most important posting houses along the mail route to London. Its livery stables were celebrated, as was the quality of the horses there. They stood at the southern end of the great Montreal wall which skirted Riverhead Square.

131 and **132** A nostalgic picture of the 1870 period showing Chipstead Lane as it left the Square at Riverhead. Taken from a stereo pair, this photo just includes, on the right, the water supply where the people of Riverhead drew their household water. Later, when steam engines were plentiful, the hole was adapted to provide water for the boilers. The hoses had to be thrown over the wall into the stream and a wooden roller was provided on the wall top so that the hoses were not damaged when being pulled back. The roller was still in place a year or so ago.

133 An incredible scene, when one realises that it is a photograph of the main London Road at Riverhead. The photographer had his back to the Bullfinch pub and was facing Sevenoaks. A shadowy Riverhead Church can be seen in the distance. The great Flemish type house was part and parcel of the tanyard on the other side of the road. One of the drying sheds can be seen on the left. Part of the building and wall still remain.

134 If you had stood in the 1870s in Riverhead Square, this is what you would have seen as you looked toward Sevenoaks. The cottage on the left was a school by the Church entrance, run by a Miss Whitehead. There, local children could be educated for two pennies each week. Behind the school, where the Memorial Hall now stands, was Miss Whitehead's father's stonemason's yard. Evidence of this still remains, for behind the present hall can be seen the wall on which the young masons practised making their personal 'marks'. In the 18th century there was a ropewalk here, at the foot of the burial ground.

135 This photograph (about 1890) gives a perfect view of the Church at Riverhead, the Dame School at the gateway and, on the right, part of the wall which contained the square to the south and formed the once impregnable boundary of Montreal. Near where the two boys are standing, two water spouts were let into the wall to provide drinking water for the local people. The water came down from the lakes above and never failed, even in a drought. Water being what it is, there were always some small boys present by the spouts.

136 This must surely be one of the best photographs of Riverhead ever to come out of the past. Oldsters will remember it well.

Here can be seen Riverhead Square from the junction of London Road and Bradbourne Vale Road. The photographer was looking towards Sevenoaks, near the old water fountain which dominated that junction for the best part of a century. Hardly any of the buildings in the picture exist today. The White Hart has gone, leaving only a parade named after it. Over the heads of the people in the street can just be seen the sign of Mr Banderet, the baker whose golden voice entertained hundreds during the First World War. In the distance is the Montreal wall and gate. Behind the trees at left, Mr Emery's hardware shop occupies most of the space. From the telegraph poles one would date this about 1900.

137 Here is the only photograph I have ever discovered of the Spouts in Riverhead Square. It was found as a 'magic lantern' slide by Miss K. Lowin of Dunton Green, who kindly allowed a copy to be made.

The Spouts provided Riverhead with sweet water for many years. The stream from which it came still flows in front of Barclay's Bank but has long been culverted. The First World War memorial which used to be over the water place now hangs outside the memorial hall.

Many old men looking at this picture will have pleasant memories of games in the square, with much of the fun coming from the Spouts' water.

139 Who could have guessed that the little building in this photograph would eventually become what it is today?

The reader may be forgiven if he fails, at first, to recognise what may be his 'local'.

It is the original Bullfinch pub on the south side of the Marley lakes. When this photograph was taken, about 1880, it was a small and popular alehouse on the corner boundary of Major F. B. Baden Powell's garden, facing the water cress beds on the corner marked by the twin telephone poles. The age of the picture is indicated by the fact that only about 10 twin lines were scheduled on the poles which had just been installed. The wires had not yet been provided.

138 Whatever the housewife of the early 1900s wanted in the way of kitchen and household goods, Mr W. Jarvis of Riverhead would supply it. He made the rounds of the district each week selling pails and brushes, paraffin and colza oil, pots and pans, brooms, mats, china and every possible kind of lamp for the home. His little shop and the large stores behind were at the foot of the entrance to the Patch, near The Bullfinch pub.

Sundridge & Brasted

140 One of the oldest photographs of Sundridge in existence. It is marked 1859 and shows the Lamb Inn and mill head-race, looking towards Bessels Green.

Such a scene, with old buildings and a large expanse of water, was often a favourite with early photographers. With no movement to contend with, and all the ingredients of an artistic picture, it was a 'natural' subject.

141 This heavy haulage is very thirsty work! At least three hauliers have temporarily abandoned the daily grind for a drink at the 'local', and their horses, with nosebags firmly fixed, are also ready to take time off.

The scene is The Lamb Inn at Sundridge in about 1900. The A25 has not yet become the busy east-west racecourse of the present day, and motor cars had not yet become the problem they were destined to be in the 1970s. The A25 of our picture is as yet unmetalled; the stream (left) was then the head-race of the mill dimly seen in the distance.

142 Looking the other way, this photographer chose the big head-race rather than the Lamb Inn for his record. A single old lady provides the 'figure' which was considered essential to conform to artistic convention.

The dirt-bound A25 had not yet been extended into the path of the stream when this was taken. There was only one nebulous footpath, but who cared. Carts were the only traffic and they were easily dodged. It is interesting to note the observation area formed by the land jutting into the river to the right of the old lady.

Due to the long exposure the child accompanying the lady has blurred into indistinction and the fast-flowing river has flattened itself so as to resemble an oily mirror.

144 A photograph of an unknown man, taken about 120 years ago as he approached the lych gate of Sundridge Church. The picture gives no clue as to the identity of the man. His name may well appear on one of the tombstones in the churchyard he was visiting so long ago.

143 A grim fortress, one might imagine. And it was; when this old photograph was taken the building, today the Sundridge Hospital, was the Ide Hill 'Spike' or workhouse where the down-and-outs lived, from day to day, doing a day's work for a bed and a meal. There was no Welfare State. If you had no money you either entered the workhouse or died.

Old people, no longer able to get work, walked from spike to spike down from London to Farnborough, then to Ide Hill and on to Guildford. In winter they sat on frozen logs breaking stones for roadmaking or picking oakum — combing the tarry tow into loose fibres which were afterwards used for caulking ships. The gardens were rich and productive. Labour cost nothing here and the produce was profitable.

145 Sundridge crossroads over a century ago. This old record, taken by the photographer Jewell of Westerham, bears the date 1860. It was taken from the entrance to the Chevening Road, looking up Church Lane with Sevenoaks to the left and Westerham to the right. Just above the shadowy figure of the cart can be seen the sign 'The Victory', and the name Harvey below. It appears to have been a public house in opposition to the White Horse, a very small piece of the latter pub can just be seen on the other side of the road.

146 Who would believe that this peaceful picture was taken on the A25 road? It shows the great east-west highway as it was when only men and horses were the users and cars were undreamed of. Despite the 19th century atmosphere, the telephone poles date the picture at about 1910. Looking towards Westerham, we see the turning to Ide Hill indicated by a finger-post.

147 Brasted village, almost 100 years ago. Little has changed in the outline of the buildings. The dark little people who were obviously recruited as models to give the picture life somehow achieve the opposite effect. They are standing outside what is now an antique print gallery, on the exact site of today's Zebra crossing.

148 Once again we look at the A25 when it was little more than a dirt track carrying horses and carriages, carts and litters. This 1875 photograph shows Brasted Green with its still familiar pump next door to the Forge and carriage works.

For generations, waggons and every kind of cart or trap, horse-bus or carriage were made by skilled craftsmen. The industry continued into this century and the era of the internal combustion engine. This photograph shows just a few of the horse-drawn vehicles turned out by this thriving 19th century factory.

149 Every few miles along the River Darent there is a mill of ancient
origin. This beautiful mill still stands on the river at Brasted, but when
this photograph was taken about 1880 the great wheel was intact and in
constant use. It can plainly be seen — a black mass against the white wall
of the mill. The origin of this mill is obscure, but it is not as ancient as
those which flourished at Longford and Chipstead, both on sites of more
ancient mills.

150 An 1866 photograph of the White Hart, Brasted, the pub which 74 years later was to become the favourite of the Battle of Britain pilots from Biggin Hill airfield. In that span, the house has altered out of all recognition and garages have replaced the two cottages that once stood on the west side.

Another thing has altered — the price of a pint. When this picture was exposed a pint of Watkins's best bitter cost 2d.

151 This photograph shows the opening of the Darent swimming pool at Brasted by Earl Stanhope. I cannot date the picture accurately; knowing that Earl Stanhope was born in 1880, and guessing that he was about 33 (from close-ups) when he performed the opening ceremony, I imagine the picture to date from around 1913. The pool was quite the coldest in Kent according to those who used it. It was closed only a few years ago to provide a little more room for the village football ground.

Westerham

152 One of the oldest photographs of Westerham, taken on a market day about 1859. It illustrates the rural character of this small market town with cattle on the green, and the un-metalled dirt road. Even in those remote times, Westerham held a particular dignity as a town, with particularly fine buildings in the area and in the High Street.

153 This old photograph, taken about 1859, has managed to catch the scene at Westerham's weekly market in an unusually 'active' way for the times. Despite the fact that the photographer had to make an exposure of at least a quarter of a minute, most of the people in the picture have remained static enough for their images to be recorded. The young man in the foreground (right) has been photographed twice because he stood still for a short time and then moved to the right. Where General Wolfe's statue now stands was then a cattle drinking trough.

154 Westerham has seen little structural change in the 120 years since this old photograph was taken. Stalls are dotted all along the High Street, and the George and Dragon does a roaring trade. Local farmers have brought their beasts in for sale while their dairy maids sell their master's butter on the Green.

155 When the fair made its regular visit to Westerham the Green was covered with gipsy caravans which housed the travellers. About the centre caravan can just be seen the roundabout with its glittering brass and traditional fairground organ. The original photograph is dated 1860.

156 This photograph, full of movement, was taken on the occasion some time in the 1860s of the return of Col. Charles Warde and his bride from their honeymoon. The people on the Green at Westerham made this an occasion of great rejoicing and welcome, even to erecting great bowers of laurel across the church gates and in the main road by the entrance to the London Road. Charles Warde married Kathleen Louisa O'Brien, thirteenth child of an Irish Peer. The marriage was at Queen's Gate in London. On this occasion the boys of Hosey School were given a day's holiday to mark the event. Charles Warde was grandfather to Mr John Warde who now farms Force Green farm.

157 It is hard to believe that the road in this century old photograph was the main road to Sevenoaks, our present A25, which carries most of the east-west traffic. The photo was made on a primitive glass plate and, in order to stop blurring, everyone in sight had to stand perfectly still for about a quarter of a minute. The road had not yet been tarred and was merely dirt, packed hard by a steam roller. Quebec House was round the corner, just out of sight.

158 This was the regular stage coach, making its daily halt outside the posting house on the south side of Westerham High Street. The journey from London, via Keston and Westerham to Guildford, took a complete day. The journey further west continued after an overnight stay in Guildford.

160 Visitors are invariably impressed by the beauty of the ancient hotel and restaurant at Moorhouse, Westerham — the Grasshopper Inn. They would still be impressed, perhaps, if they knew that the whole building was modern and started from these two cottages — one of which was a tiny rural pub called the Grasshopper. The present building was erected by Bill Newman, architect of a similar place in Dunton Green, Donnington Manor (see caption **125**). The photograph was taken about 1863.

159 This little corner of Westerham has seen much change since the turn of the century. When M. Jewell, or perhaps Mr F.G. Benson, took this picture the old forge was still standing, and the shop on the extreme right was then a sweetshop. A few paces beyond the camera would have opened the view of the Long Pond shown in picture **162**.

161 A 'scoop' photograph which I took of Sir Winston Churchill, just after the war when Chartwell grounds caught fire, causing great damage to the rhododendrons which were a feature there. Sir Winston, in his wartime siren suit, posed especially for this picture after being discovered putting out the fire by natural means. It was a reward for my discretion in not having recorded the event.

162 This beautiful rural picture was taken by Mr F.G. Benson, the Westerham photographer, artist and taxidermist. It shows the Long Pond, opposite the Westerham Brewery on the road to Limpsfield. At that time (about 1890) this was a most beautiful area to which drivers brought their carts in order to wash them. In winter time the long pond was a mecca for skaters of all ages. Today, the pond has all but disappeared in water weed, rushes and silt.